GW00381670

Village Walks
in
DORSET

For Marie and Edward

Village Walks
in
DORSET

Anne-Marie Edwards

COUNTRYSIDE BOOKS
NEWBURY, BERKSHIRE

First published 1998
© Anne-Marie Edwards 1998

COUNTRYSIDE BOOKS
3 Catherine Road
Newbury, Berkshire

ISBN 1 85306 495 5

Designed by Graham Whiteman
Photographs by Mike Edwards
Maps and illustrations by Trevor Yorke

Produced through MRM Associates Ltd., Reading
Printed by Woolnough Bookbinding Ltd., Irthlingborough

Contents

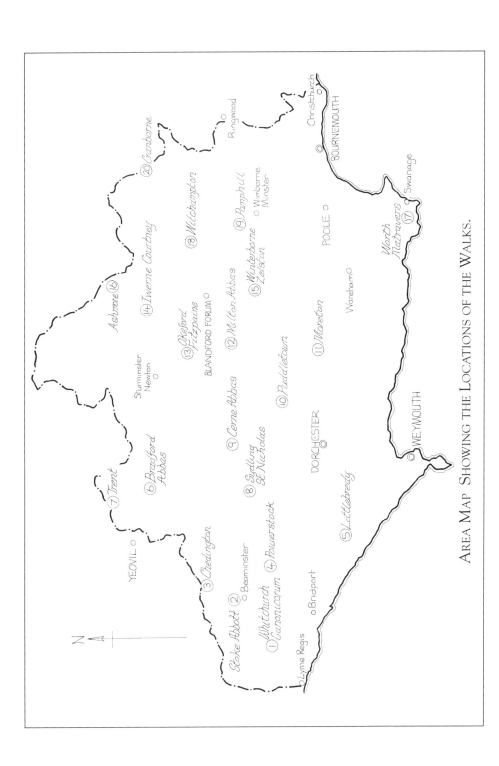

AREA MAP SHOWING THE LOCATIONS OF THE WALKS.

WALK

Acknowledgements

I am most grateful to Edward and Marie Swann who helped me with the research and shared with me their love of Dorset. As always I thank Mary and Ken Chambers for their never-failing support, and the staff of Southampton and Totton libraries. My thanks also to my husband Mike whose many duties include accompanying me on the walks, taking the photographs, performing miracles with map and compass and sharing the fun of writing this book. I would also like to thank Paula Leigh and all my friends at Countryside Books for helping to make writing this book such a pleasure.

Publisher's Note

We hope that you obtain considerable enjoyment from this book; great care has been taken in its preparation. Although at the time of publication all routes followed public rights of way or permitted paths, diversion orders can be made and permissions withdrawn.

We cannot of course be held responsible for such diversion orders and any inaccuracies in the text which result from these or any other changes to the routes nor any damage which might result from walkers trespassing on private property. We are anxious though that all details covering the walks are kept up to date and would therefore welcome information from readers which would be relevant to future editions.

Introduction

To walk in Dorset is to step back in time. This small county is rural England at its most tranquil and unchanging. Here you will find a peaceful landscape of great interest and beauty crossed by no major roads, with little industry and few large towns, where life moves at the pace of the walker rather than the car. There is time in Dorset for neighbours to chat and for visitors to be made welcome. Admire a garden and you will be invited in for tea!

Although Dorset is a small county you will discover an amazing variety of scenery. It has been said that after a tour of the county you will have seen three-quarters of England! Forming the heart of Dorset is a great range of chalk downs through which the main rivers, the Cerne, the Frome, the Piddle, the Stour and the Allen have carved narrow valleys on their way to meet the sea at Poole Harbour. North of the downs is Cranborne Chase, once a hunting forest and still a splendid area for the walker. West of the Chase lies the enchanting Vale of Blackmoor, with its gently undulating landscape, high-hedged lanes and flower-filled meadows. South of the downs the hills give way to a magnificent coastline running east from Lyme Regis past the Isle of Purbeck, famous for its wildlife, to Christchurch. In the west of the county Dorset's highest hills, Pilsdon Pen, Lewesdon and Eggardon, encircle the mysterious Marshwood Vale.

History lies round every corner. The summits of the hills are ringed with the embankments of Neolithic camps and Iron Age forts and south of Dorchester rises the mighty fort of Maiden Castle dating back nearly six thousand years. The people of the Bronze Age have left their trading routes, and medieval farmers have scored the hillsides with strip lynchets. The quiet valleys have attracted Christian settlements from earliest times adding 'Abbas' to the names of several Dorset villages. North of Blandford Forum, close to the village of Iwerne Courtney, a group of local men tired of the unrest caused by the Civil War, defied Cromwell on Hambledon Hill, and Charles II sought sanctuary at Trent, near the border with Somerset, after his defeat at the battle of Worcester.

The villages of Dorset are as varied and charming as its scenery. They are far enough apart to have different characters yet they could belong to no other county. Many roofs are dark-thatched but walls can be built from whatever local materials came to hand from humble cob to the glowing honey-coloured stone from Ham Hill seen in many villages in the west of the county. In the Purbecks whole villages are built and roofed with stone from local quarries. Many Dorset villages preserve fascinating hints of the past: the scalloped steps of an ancient preaching cross, medieval wall paintings, mills which ground grain before the Conqueror. Local activities flourish in even the smallest communities with church and manor still playing an important part in village life.

All the villages are surrounded by footpaths shaped by the needs of its people: old ways followed in the course of their everyday lives, to work, to church, to the nearest inn, to visit friends. If you follow in their footsteps you will discover the unique charm of each village as well as the beauty of the countryside which surrounds it.

The lifeblood of any village is its inhabitants, and Dorset villagers care for their lovely environment. Therefore, we are asked to respect the villagers' way of life and to use the utmost discretion when parking vehicles. Car parking locations are indicated in the text – but if they are full, or for some reason unusable, please ensure that you park your vehicle in such a way as not to be a nuisance to those who live close by.

All the walks in this book are circular and suitable for the family. They range in length from 3 to 7 miles and are accompanied by simple sketch maps designed to guide you to the starting point and give an overall picture of the route. For more detailed information I recommend you arm yourself with the relevant Ordnance Survey Landranger map noted in the introduction to each walk. The Pathfinder maps at 1:25 000 are even better, but as each covers such a small area you may need two for some of the walks. Places where food and drink can be obtained are also given for each walk, together with the relevant telephone numbers so that opening times can be checked.

Finally I wish you many happy hours exploring this enchanting county. I hope you will derive as much pleasure from using this book as I have in writing it.

Anne-Marie Edwards

WHITCHURCH CANONICORUM

Length: 4½ miles

Getting there: Whitchurch Canonicorum lies just north of the A35 between Charmouth and Bridport. Approaching from the east, turn right, following the sign for Ryall. The lane bears right then winds uphill through Ryall to Whitchurch Canonicorum. Pass the Five Bells Inn on the left and after a few yards there is a parking area on the right before the road curves left. Approaching from the west, turn left following the sign for Whitchurch Canonicorum. Drive past the church. The road continues uphill. Just before a right-hand bend, you will see the parking area on the left.

Parking: In the parking area described.

Map: OS Landranger 193. (GR 398953).

The Marshwood Vale is one of Dorset's secret places. The undulating landscape, crossed by a network of narrow, high-hedged lanes and dotted with isolated farmsteads, is almost entirely surrounded by hills. Northwards the Vale is dominated by the heights of Pilsdon Pen and Lewesdon and to the south rise the steep slopes of the coastal hills. The capital of this secluded world, overlooking the vale's southern fringe, is Whitchurch Canonicorum. Once important enough to be included in the will of King Alfred, it is now just a tranquil cluster of old-world houses grouped around a magnificent church which holds a unique treasure. The church of St Candida and the Holy Cross is the only parish church in England to possess the relics of its patron saint, in this case Saint Wite, latinised as Candida.

Throughout the Middle Ages all paths across the Vale led to her shrine and this walk follows some of these ancient ways. The route takes a riverside path along the Char valley then climbs to follow a ridge affording splendid views before returning to Whitchurch Canonicorum.

THE WALK

❶ From the parking area turn down a narrow, high-hedged footpath which leads past a thatched house on the right towards the church tower in the distance. (Ignore

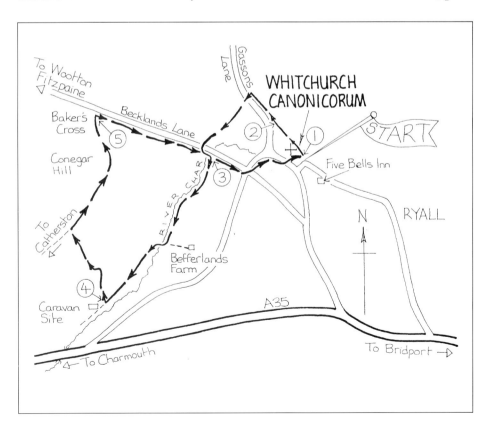

The valley of the Char.

the bridleway signed 'Stoke Mandeville'.) When the path divides keep ahead (right-hand path) towards the tower. Before you reach the gate leading into the churchyard look for a stile on the right. Cross the stile, then bear left to follow the hedge round to the point where it turns left. With the church tower now behind you keep straight ahead over the field to cross a stile. A clear path leads a little left down the field. Cross the next stile and still bearing a little left, cross the field to a gate opening into Gassons Lane.

❷ Turn right and follow the lane over a bridge. Immediately over the bridge look for a gate on the left and footpath sign 'To Charmouth'. Turn left and follow the field path towards a gate in the opposite hedge.

Bear left just before the gate and continue with the hedge on your right to a stile on the right. Cross and bear left over a narrow field. When this widens, keep ahead aiming to walk to the right of some tall poplar trees to meet Becklands Lane. Turn left for a few yards to cross the river Char.

❸ Immediately after the bridge look carefully for a stile on the right. Cross, and follow paths over fields and stiles, keeping

---

PLACES of INTEREST

Two miles south of Whitchurch Canonicorum, at Morecombelake, visitors are welcome to look round **Moore's biscuit factory**, home of the famous 'Dorset Knobs'. Open Monday to Friday from 9 am to 5 pm. Telephone: 01297 89253.

the river close on your right. After a stile indicating another footpath to the left keep ahead close to the river bank, ignoring a more obvious path bearing left. Go through a small gate and follow a narrow path through trees with the river close on your right. Bear left over a small wooden bridge, cross the stile, and bear right to continue heading for Charmouth for about 30 yards. Turn right, cross another stile and small bridge and resume your heading with the river still on your right. Cross a further small bridge and stile and continue over the next stile to a crosstrack. Befferlands farmhouse is on the hillside on the left. Turn right over a wide bridge to cross the Char. Go through the gate and up the meadow towards another gate. Bear left before the gate and with the river now on your left continue to a stile with a caravan park just beyond.

❹ Do not cross the stile but turn right to climb the hillside, hedge on left. Cross a stile and walk uphill to cross another stile. Continue for about 200 yards and look for a gap in the hedge with a narrow earth path running through it. Turn left along the

path to cross a stile and bear right up a narrow path, hedge on right, fence on left. Cross a stile and keep on uphill over a stile to a crosspath running just below the crest of the hill.

Turn right to walk along the ridge path with beautiful views of the Marshwood Vale on your left and the valley of the Char on your right. Continue through gates and over the track for Wootton Fitz-paine, following the sign for Baker's Cross. The path rises to curve round the shoulder of wooded Conegar Hill, at its loveliest in spring when the ground is carpeted with wild daffodils. Leave the woods through a gate and follow the field path to meet Becklands Lane at Baker's Cross.

❺ Turn right to descend the lane, signed 'Whitchurch', to a crossroads in Whitchurch Canonicorum. Turn left (signed 'To the Church') through the village. Turn left at the memorial cross towards the church gates. Follow the narrow footpath to the right of the gates to join the path you followed at the start of the walk. Turn right to walk up to the parking area.

STOKE ABBOTT

Length: 4 miles

Getting there: Stoke Abbott is about 6 miles north of Bridport. It is signed off the B3162, the Broadwindsor road.	**Parking:** Drive into the village and park on the left just after a lane on the left signed for Broadwindsor.	**Map:** OS Landranger 193. (GR 453008).

Stoke Abbott is enchantingly pretty. Tucked deep in a hollow among the West Dorset hills, the thatched golden-stone houses seem lost among green knolls and copse woods. Dominating the north of the village is Waddon Hill crowned with the embankments of a fort built by the Romans during the invasion of AD 43. A mile to the west is Lewesdon Hill, beautifully wooded with massive beech trees and at almost 900 feet one of Dorset's highest hills.

The walk from this lovely village leads to a green plateau on the top of Lewesdon Hill where you will enjoy a magnificent view south over the pastoral Marchwood Vale to the coastal hills ringed by the sea and inland over rural Dorset and the Somerset Levels. On the way the path climbs through the ancient beech woods for which Lewesdon is famous and after a steep descent quiet paths and lanes lead back to the village.

THE WALK

❶ From the parking area in Stoke Abbott turn up the lane signed for Broadwindsor. The sunken lane climbs steadily towards Stoke Knap on the top of Waddon Hill. Pass the turning on the left in front of Stoke Knap Cottage and continue up the hill. At the top, opposite Stoke Knap Farm, bear left to cross the main road and take the track on the left signed with the green arrow of the Wessex Ridgeway.

❷ Follow the track which runs high along a ridge already affording splendid views. As the way approaches Lewesdon, it becomes a green sunken track leading gradually up through avenues of silver trunked beeches, their tangled roots rising above the earth and twisted into fantastic shapes. Keep ahead to a crosspath.

❸ Turn left to follow the path uphill through the trees to the highest point on Lewesdon. The path levels as it crosses the grassy summit and now you can enjoy the

reward for your climb – the stunning view! The loaf-shaped hill rising to the west is Pilsdon Pen, the highest hill in Dorset. Ahead the coastal range dips to form the valley of the river Char and a little to the left of it you will see the distinctive outline of Golden Cap.

The path now drops steeply down the hill. Keep ahead with an embankment surmounted by beech trees close on your left. At the foot of the hill go through an iron gate to a concrete track. Turn left and after about 30 yards you will see a gate on your right.

❹ Turn right through the gate. Two paths lead across the field ahead. Ignore the more obvious path straight ahead and take the left-hand path. Go through a gateway at the other side of the field and keep straight ahead over the next field, (there may be no clear path at this point). Go through the gate to a lane. Turn left and follow the lane to the crossroads at Four Ashes. Cross the main road, the B3162, and follow the lane ahead signed for Stoke Abbott. The lane leads to Brimley Farm. Bear right in front of the farm to a footpath on the left. Follow this over two stiles to a meadow where there is no clear path. Walk down the field (indicated by a Jubilee Trail arrow) keeping

The spring in Stoke Abbott was given a lion's head in 1953. An iron drinking cup is fastened beside it.

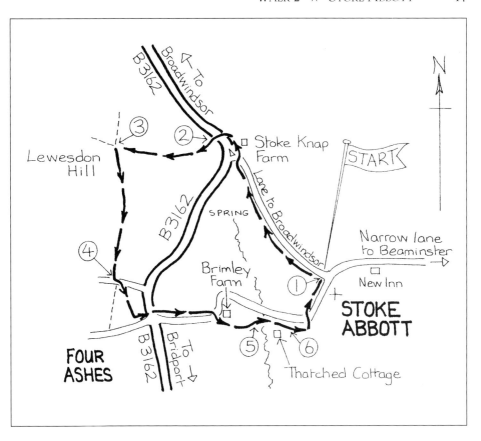

a hedge close on your right to a post marked with several signs.

❺ At the post turn left (indicated by another Jubilee Trail arrow). You will see a thatched cottage on the hillside on your right and we are aiming for a track to the left of it. Walk down the steep hillside to a stile and cross the small wooden bridge over a stream. Bear a little left to cross another stile. Turn left to climb up the field and now bear a little right to a stile in the fence ahead. The thatched cottage overlooking a lake in the valley is over the field on your right. Cross a track, climb the steps ahead and go over the stile.

❻ Keep straight ahead over the field, go through a gap in the hedge and over the next field, bearing right to go through a gateway to a track at the approach to Stoke Abbott. Turn left to walk down to the road which runs through the village. Turn right to walk through the village past the church to the parking area by the lane for Broadwindsor.

CHEDINGTON

Length: 4½ miles

Getting there: Chedington is in north-west Dorset about 6 miles north of Beaminster. The best approach is from the A356 Crewkerne to Maiden Newton road. Turn for Chedington

beside the Winyard's Gap Inn.

Parking: After passing the inn continue along the lane for Chedington for ¼ mile. As you approach the village there is

room to park beside a stone wall on the right just before a lane on the left signed for Mosterton.

Maps: OS Landrangers 193 and 194. (GR 489057).

Chedington is a beautiful and most unusual village. A single street of houses and cottages, mostly built of golden Ham Hill stone, clings to the side of a steep ridge, shadowed by venerable beech trees. Gardens provide brilliant splashes of colour among the trees and every wall is graced with roses and climbing plants. From the village street there are breathtaking views westwards over the valley of the Parrett to the Somerset hills.

From the village, the route climbs the ridge then leads along the top through the beech trees to the memorial to the men o

---

FOOD and DRINK

Winyard's Gap Inn offers a wide range of excellent food. The fish menu is particularly impressive. Opening times are from 11.30 am to 2.30 pm and from 7 pm to 11 pm. Meals are served from 12 noon to 1.45 pm and from 7 pm to 9 pm. Telephone: 01935 891244.

---

the 43rd (Wessex) Division of the Dorset-shire Regiment who fell during their first major battle in the Normandy Campaign in July 1944. The stone is a replica of the one on Point 112, the hill 5 miles south-west of Caen where the battle was fought. Looking east from the memorial you enjoy a splendid view over the undulating Dorset countryside as far as the dark slopes of the North Downs. After descending the ridge by the Winyard's Gap Inn the walk follows lanes and grassy paths through the peaceful Corscombe Valley passing Crook Hill, a lovely area of unimproved grassland dotted with mature oaks in the care of the National Trust.

THE WALK

❶ Walk into the village, leaving the turning to Mosterton on your left. The large house behind the wall on your right is Chedington Court built in the 1890s. Opposite stands Manor Farm, a charming house with mullioned windows and firmly buttressed walls. Above the porch is the date 1634. Follow the lane past the church, now a private house. The lane bends left to pass rows of thatched cottages. When the lane divides, bear left and walk up the hill to meet a road. Turn left along the road which runs along the top of the ridge with the rooftops of Chedington village below the beech trees on your left and fine views east and west.

❷ Pass a lane on the left but turn left down the next lane, signed 'Chedington'. A few yards down the lane look for a National Trust sign, 'Winyard's Gap', and a narrow path on the right. Turn right up the path and when it divides keep to the left-hand path which dips then climbs to follow the top of the ridge through the woods. Keep your height, following the left shoulder of the ridge as the path passes other narrow ways on the right. Still keeping to the main path, follow it as it gradually descends, bearing left then right to meet a crosspath almost at the foot of the hillside. On the left the path runs through a small wooden gate to a parking area beside the road.

❸ At the crosspath turn right to climb to the memorial, then retrace your steps downhill to go through the wooden gate to the road. Turn right past the Winyard's Gap Inn on the right, cross the A356, and follow the lane ahead, signed 'Halstock'. At the division in front of Pretty Box Farm bear right. The quiet lane winds past loaf-shaped Crook Hill on the left which you may like to explore before continuing with the walk. After about ½ mile look for a blue arrow bridleway sign by a gate on the right.

❹ Bear left through the gate along the edge of a field, fence on left. Continue through two more gates, keeping a hedge on the left. Go through the next gate and keep to the path as it curves downhill away from the hedge to join a farm track and bear right over a small stream. Follow the track uphill and over a field to a gate with a barn on the right. Go through the gate and

In the Corscombe valley.

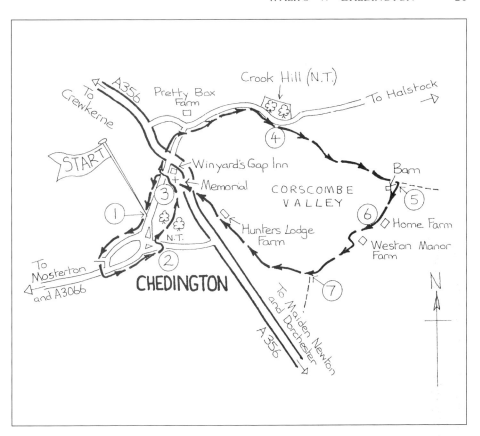

just past the barn turn right, following the blue sign.

❺ Keep ahead past more barns to continue along a lane leaving the entrance to Weston Manor on your left. Follow the lane past Home Farm, leaving all the farm buildings on your left. A hedged path now leads towards Weston Manor Farm.

❻ Navigate carefully here! Do not go through the gate into the farmyard, but just before it, turn right through another gate and follow the path round the farm,

leaving all the buildings on your left. When the path rejoins the track bear right. Follow the attractive grassy path ahead which leads along the valley to two bridleway signs.

❼ Ignore the path straight ahead and turn right through a gate to follow the path past Hunter's Lodge Farm. The path becomes a lane and crosses two cattle grids before meeting the A356. Turn right beside the road for about 100 yards and turn left just past the Winyard's Gap Inn to follow the lane into Chedington.

POWERSTOCK

Length: 4½ miles

Getting there: Powerstock is 4 miles north-east of Bridport. From Bridport take the A3066 (for Beaminster) and turn right, following the signs for Powerstock.

Parking: Drive into the village and park in the Square near the church.

Map: OS Landranger 194. (GR 517962)

When the BBC wished to make a documentary about a village least changed by the 20th century they chose Powerstock! Approached by sunken lanes, the village lies deep in a wooded cleft among the rounded chalk hills of West Dorset. From its vantage point high on a hill the church overlooks a scattering of golden-stone houses, mostly thatched, set among winding streams, colourful gardens and overgrown orchards. Powerstock is a working village still. Cows wander over the Square to the farm close to the church at milking time, there is a blacksmith and a flourishing village school. A visit to the church is a must! The 15th-century south

From the village, the walk climbs a quiet country lane to the top of the downs revealing wide views over an enchanting landscape. The route then follows a path along a remote valley to the little hamlet of West Milton beside the Mangerton river. Meadow paths close to the river lead us back to Powerstock. In midsummer the meadows are brilliant with wild flowers and alive with butterflies.

doorway is richly carved with figures set in canopied niches and the chancel has one of the finest Norman arches in Dorset, decorated with zig-zags and rope tracery. In the churchyard is a 13th-century stone dole table where loaves were once placed for distribution to the poor.

THE WALK

❶ The walk starts from the Square in front of the church where five roads meet. Do not take any of the signed roads, but

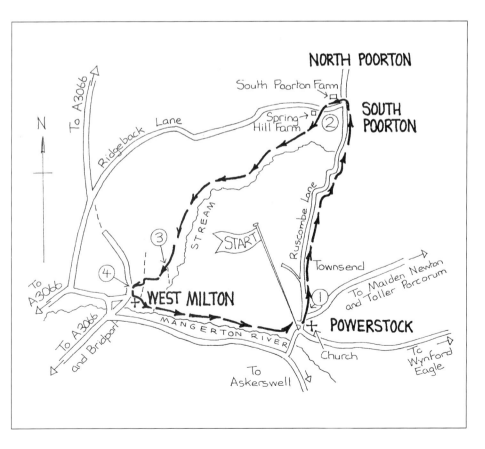

Looking towards Eggardon Hill from West Milton churchyard.

with the church tower on your right and the lane marked with a 'no through road' sign on your left cross the road signed for Maiden Newton and walk up the unsigned lane ahead. (It is due north - you can check the direction by the weathercock on the church tower.) The lane climbs past the entrance to an impressive house guarded by stone lions. Pass the sign 'Townsend' and when the lane divides bear half-right to continue uphill. The lane descends to pass the track to Poorton Hill Farm, crosses a stream, then climbs once more to pass Bottom Farm and continue uphill to a T-junction opposite South Poorton Farm.

❷ Turn left to leave South Poorton Farm on your right and follow the lane as it bears right past Poorton House. The lane curves right and you will see a sign for Spring Hill Farm on the left. Just before the sign look for a narrow footpath marked with a yellow arrow. The path may be a little overgrown at this point but becomes easy to follow within a few yards. Turn left to leave Spring Hill Farm on your right and descend to a sunken path leading down the valley. For about 30 yards the path may be wet as a small stream runs close by but then the path becomes a pleasant tree-shaded walk with the stream taking its own route on your left. Cross a stile to continue along the valley with glimpses of open hillsides through the trees on your right. The path now leads into open meadowland as it traces the side of this lovely valley. The only sounds you will hear are the babbling of the stream beneath its canopy of beech and oak and perhaps the mewing of buzzards wheeling overhead. Turn left over the next stile to continue with a fence on

your left. Go through a gate and keep ahead to walk between tall trees. The path bears a little left downhill to cross two stiles. Keep ahead over the hillside to go through a gate and continue through a wooded area. The path emerges to follow the hillside again. Over the next stile the path runs at first beside trees on the left. As you reach the open hillside once more look across the valley to see the opposite hillside heavily scored with strip lynchets.

❸ Go through an iron gate and after a few yards follow the right hand of the two narrow paths ahead which soon bears a little right over the meadow to cross a stile and meet a crosstrack. Turn left to go through a gate and follow a track to the road in West Milton.

❹ Turn left along the road for only a few yards and look carefully for a flight of steps on the left. Turn left up the steps. On your right stands a 15th-century tower, all that remains of an ancient chapel. The nave and chancel were demolished after 1873. Keep ahead through a gap in the stone wall. Now you have a magnificent view of Eggardon Hill crowned with its triple-banked Iron Age hill fort rising against the

---

PLACES of INTEREST

Drive to the top of **Eggardon Hill**, crowned with a magnificent Iron Age hill fort, towering 800 feet to the south-east of Powerstock. From here you can enjoy a splendid view over the Marshwood Vale. **Mangerton Mill**, 3 miles west of Powerstock off the B3066, is a 17th-century working watermill. Refreshments are available. Opening times vary. Telephone: 01308 85321 for details.

The medieval dole table in Powerstock churchyard. Loaves would have been placed here for distribution to the poor.

skyline. Cross the stile and keep ahead over the meadows, following the blue bridleway sign to go through a wooden gate and over a small bridge. Through the next gate keep to the lower of two tracks which rises to go through another wooden gate. A clear way now leads through coppiced hazels, bearing left to reveal Powerstock in the valley on the right. The path curves left then right to lead down to the village. Turn right to walk up to the church.

LITTLEBREDY

Length: 6 miles

Getting there: Littlebredy lies just south of the A35 between Dorchester and Bridport. Approaching from Dorchester, drive through Winterbourne Abbas and after about a mile turn left, following the sign for Littlebredy 1½ miles.

Parking: Follow the lane into the valley and keep to the lane as it bears right past two private roads on the left. Immediately after the second you will see a six-sided shelter with a pyramid-shaped roof on the left. The official parking area is on the left just past the shelter.

Map: OS Landranger 194. (GR 587880).

Hidden deep in a wooded valley surrounded by high downland, Littlebredy is a magical place. No traffic disturbs this tranquil cluster of thatched cottages at the entrance to the gardens surrounding Bridehead, a great house built in classical style in the early 19th century. Although the house is private, a kindly notice invites visitors to walk and picnic in the gardens free of charge and suggests that a contribution could be put in the church box.

Littlebredy is at the source of the river Bride which runs to the sea through a wide green valley with tiny villages folded in the hills. The walk climbs high to follow the crest of the downs giving marvellous views over the valley to the sea glinting in the distance, dominated by Golden Cap, the highest cliff on the south coast. These downs were cultivated by the first farmers in the New Stone Age and the route passes one of their burial chambers, known as the Grey Mare and her Colts. Later, about 4,000 years ago, Bronze Age people lived and held celebrations here and close to the route of the walk you will see one of their henge monuments, the Kingston Russell stone circle.

THE WALK

❶ Pass the six-sided shelter on your right and turn right down the lane (the notice 'Private Road' only applies to cars). Just past the first thatched house on the left turn left through a wooden gate along an enchanting path past more thatched cottages to the church. Follow the path running a little downhill to the gardens of Bridehead to enjoy a ramble by the lake. Retrace your steps to the church, climb the steps to the porch, bear right to leave the church on your left and go through a small wooden gate to a road.

❷ Bear right along the valley road, leaving the phone box on your left. Over a crosstrack you descend to a bridleway sign

on the right. Turn right along a grassy path which curves right then leads up the down ahead. Now you have a splendid view of Bridehead over the meadows on the right. Go through a gateway and keep straight ahead uphill – ignore the track curving right. The terraced path bears left beneath some trees as it ascends the hillside. A slight left curve brings you to the right of a wooded area. Keep the woods close on your right to pass some farm buildings and go through metal gates to meet a track.

❸ Bear a little right to follow this track along the crest of the downs for about ½ mile. Ahead, over the coastal ridge, is the dark shadow of Portland and the Chesil Bank sheltering the Fleet.

❹ When the track turns left, turn right, following the sign 'Kingston Russell Stone Circle'. After about ¼ mile the path descends slightly to a hedge. Just past the hedge turn left over a stile. Keep ahead for about 100 yards to a gate on the left. Go through the gate to see the massive sarsen stones guarding the entrance to the Grey Mare and her Colts. Retrace your steps and continue the walk for about ¾ mile.

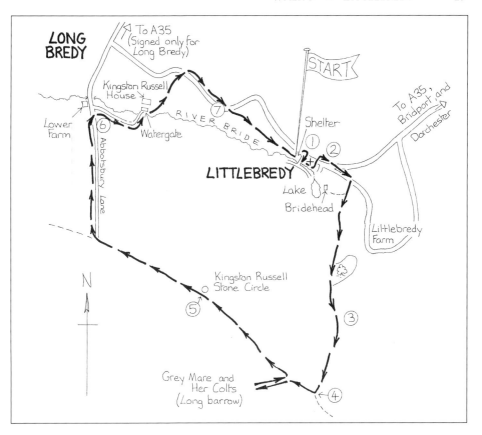

5 Go through a gate into a field. On the right you will see the fallen stones of Kingston Russell stone circle. Pass the stones and follow the path downhill. After about ¾ mile Abbotsbury Lane joins our path on the right. Turn right to follow the lane down into the valley as far as Lower Farm. The village ahead is Long Bredy.

6 Turn right opposite the farm following the sign for Kingston Russell. The lane leads to a T-junction by a cottage. Turn left for Watergate. The narrow metalled drive leads to an idyllic spot — a small bridge over the river Bride in front of some charming cottages at the gates of Kingston Russell House. Turn right in front of the cottages and go through a gate into a meadow. Keep a stone wall, later a hedge, close on your left and follow the path as it leads gently uphill towards a prominent light-coloured house. Go through a gate to a road and turn right. Continue for about ⅓ mile.

7 Just past some trees on the right you will see a stile. Turn right over the stile and bear left parallel with the road with a hedge on your left. Aim for the house you will see over the fields ahead. Look downhill a

The Grey Mare and her Colts, a Neolithic burial chamber.

little to your right and you will see two
stiles. Cross both stiles, walk up the field
and, keeping the house directly ahead,
cross another stile. The path drops
downhill to bring you to a stile leading to
the lane in Littlebredy. Turn left up the
lane to the shelter and turn left for your car.

BRADFORD ABBAS

Length: 4½ miles

Getting there: Bradford Abbas
lies beside the river Yeo, about 3
miles south east of Yeovil.
Approaching from the south,
cross the river Yeo and take the
next turning on the left – about
50 yards after crossing the river

– signed for Bradford Abbas and
the village hall. Approaching
from the north, heading south
from the Yeovil-Sherborne road,
the A30, cross the railway and
after about 100 yards turn right.
The road leads to the church

which is on the right.

Parking: There is room to park
near the church.

Map: OS Landranger 194.
(GR 587143).

Bradford Abbas is one of Dorset's most
beautiful villages, built of golden Ham Hill
stone and surrounded by gardens and
orchards that merge imperceptibly into the
countryside. The village is quiet today but
in the 15th century the wool trade brought
prosperity and the magnificent church of
St Mary dates from that time. The west
front of the tower is superb, its four storeys
surmounted by an embossed parapet and
decorated with eleven canopied niches,
two of which contain their original figures.
Inside, too, there is much to admire
including delicately carved bench ends, a

FOOD and DRINK

The Rose and Crown serves food all the week, lunches from 12 noon to 3 pm and dinners from 6.30 pm to 11 pm (7 pm to 10.30 pm on Sundays). The pub dates from the 15th century and has a magnificent stone fireplace. Telephone: 01935 74506.

Choose a day in late spring or summer if you can for this walk through the rich countryside of the Blackmoor Vale. The route follows meadow paths and lanes bordered with flowers and shaded by the great trees for which the Vale is famous. Part of the way follows the banks of the river Yeo and affords a glimpse of the Tudor manor at Clifton Maybank.

15th-century stone rood screen and a fine Jacobean pulpit.

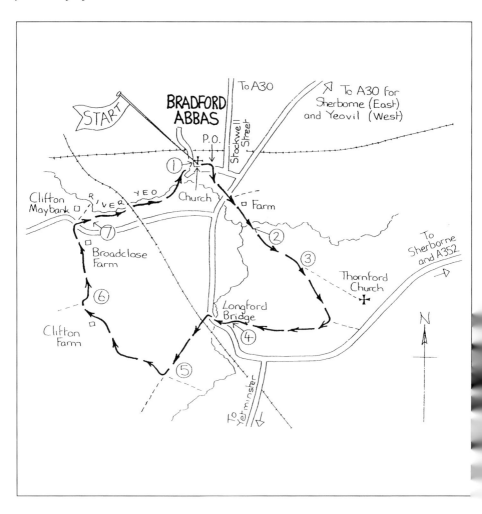

The magnificent 15th-century tower of Bradford Abbas church with two stone figures still in their original niches.

THE WALK

❶ Leaving the south front of the church on your left, walk down the village street past the Rose and Crown inn. Opposite the post office you will see a narrow path running between stone walls on your right. Turn right to step over an iron stile and follow the path which leads through a small gate to meadows bordering the river Yeo. Bear left with a stone wall at first close on your left. Go through a gate to a road. Cross straight over. Take the right hand of the two tracks you will see ahead which leads to a farm. Bear right in front of the farmhouse and go through a wooden gate which opens into the meadows. Turn immediately left along a raised path beside a small stream. The path bears a little right to cross a bridge over a tributary of the Yeo.

❷ Follow the narrow path leading across the field directly ahead. You will see the tower of Thornford church on the hill in the distance a little to your left. Cross a stile and keep straight ahead, aiming for the church tower, to a small iron gate.

❸ Go through the gate but do not continue towards the church. Turn right to walk beside the field for about 30 yards and go through a gate on the right to meet a track. Bear left and continue along the track with fields sloping up to Thornford village on your left. When the track turns left uphill, bear right along a wide green way. This well hedged and ditched path is wide enough to have been part of an old drove road. After about ½ mile the way becomes overgrown with trees but a narrow path snakes through the woods to bring you to a road.

❹ Turn right beside the road for a few yards then bear left to cross Longford Bridge over the Yeo. A few yards further on you come to a track on the left leading under a railway bridge. Turn left to follow this track which becomes asphalted running between lawns golden with daffodils in spring. In less than ½ mile you come to a crosstrack.

❺ Turn right to follow a track through an iron gate and continue beside a field to go through another gate. Keep ahead with a hedge on your right. Keep to the track as it bears right through a gate towards Clifton Farm. Pass Clifton Farm on your left. Just past the farm you will see a footpath sign on the left. Bear right over the field as the sign directs to a track. Turn right for a few yards to rejoin the track and turn left to resume your original northerly heading.

❻ Follow the lane past Broadclose Farm to a road. Bear left along the road for about 100 yards. Before the road rises and turns left, turn right through an entry to two wooden gates.

❼ Do not go through the gate directly ahead. Our way is through the right-hand gate. There is no clear path at this point but bear half-left over the grass towards a line of trees. These border the Yeo. If you look back you will see Clifton Maybank manor house on the hillside. This is the

---

PLACES of INTEREST

The historic town of **Sherborne** is within easy driving distance.

remains of a much larger mansion built by the Horsey family about 1586. When you reach the river bank follow the narrow path with the river close on your left for about ¾ mile under the left hand of two viaducts to an iron bridge. Turn left over the bridge, climb the path ahead and turn right to follow a track into Bradford Abbas. Turn left when you reach the road to return to the church and your car.

TRENT
Length: 4 miles

Getting there: Trent lies 2 miles north of the A30 between Yeovil and Sherborne. Take the turning signed for Over Compton and at the crossroads keep ahead, signed 'Trent'. After about a mile turn right for Trent.

Parking: Pass Trent church and Chantry House on the left and turn left immediately after to park just past the church gate and Manor House entrance.

Map: OS Landranger 183. (GR 590186).

In north-west Dorset, close to the border with Somerset, is a cluster of exceptionally attractive villages. One of the loveliest is Trent. Approached by quiet lanes, the village rambles through the meadows of a secluded valley just west of a range of limestone hills. Most of the houses were built of this local stone before the end of the 17th century and vary in colour from pale gold to deep russet. Little seems to have changed in Trent since Charles II fleeing from the Parliament troops after his defeat at the battle of Worcester, was hidden by Sir Francis Wyndham in the

screen carved in the 15th century, pre-Reformation pews and a finely-carved Dutch pulpit dating from around 1600. Rusted helmets and gauntlets hang over the effigies in the manorial chapel. Beside the church is the Chantry, a priest's house built in the reign of Henry VI.

Manor by the church. The church of St Andrew has a magnificent vaulted rood

From the church, the walk explores the village then follows meadow paths and

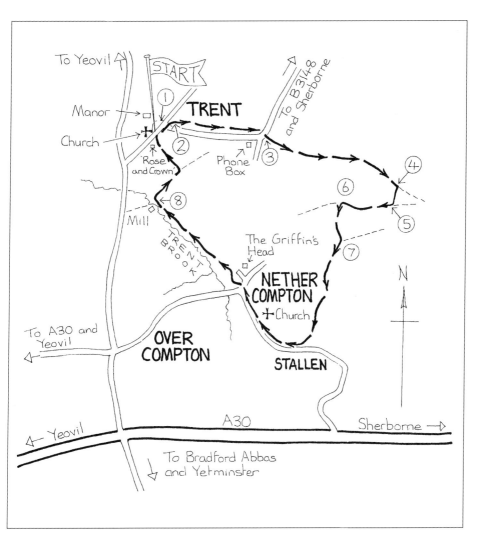

Trent church has preserved its magnificent 15th-century rood screen.

lanes to the top of the range of hills to give wide views. The route includes another interesting village before returning by field paths to Trent.

THE WALK

❶ With the entrance to the Manor on your right go through the church gate to cross the churchyard. Pass the Chantry on the left. After visiting the church retrace your steps past the Manor entrance on your left and follow the raised flagged footpath straight on up the lane. Just past Turner's Close – an attractive group of almshouses built in Tudor style clustered around a small courtyard – turn right to follow the footpath through the village.

❷ Keep to the flagged footpath past

the post office and village stores and picturesque Abel's Lane on the left. Continue through the village, still following the path, past a phone box on the right. About 100 yards further on the lane bends left.

❸ Do not follow the lane but keep straight on, following the bridleway sign. Asphalted at first, then grassy, the track runs between high hedges festooned with honeysuckle and fringed with cow parsley for much of the year. Ahead rise green hillsides with small patches of woodland dotted in the hollows. Follow the track, bearing a little right as indicated by a blue arrow bridleway sign as it rises to cross meadows and enter a wooded area.

❹ Continue past a bridleway sign on the left indicating a path up the hill and turn right to continue to a crosstrack.

❺ Turn right to follow the path along the foot of the hillside for about ¼ mile to a path on the left leading steeply uphill.

❻ Bear left to climb the hill. The climb is quite steep but short! As you near the top you are rewarded by glorious views west over Somerset. Trent, distinguished by its church spire – one of very few in Dorset – lies half-hidden by trees in its remote valley. Yeovil, little more than a mile away across the county boundary, seems to belong to a different world. The path leads over the top of the hill then descends to a crosstrack.

❼ Turn right and continue along the main track as it turns left and becomes a deep sunken lane dropping downhill to meet a lane in Stallen. Bear right to follow the lane through Nether Compton, another attractive village built of glowing local stone. Continue ahead past the turning to Over Compton along the lane signed 'no through road'. In front of the pub, the Griffin's Head, turn left to Crossways where you will see two footpath signs for Trent. Keep straight on, following 'Bridleway Trent Mill ½'. Follow this pleasant track which runs to the right of Trent Brook.

❽ The path meets a lane beside Trent Mill. Turn right up the lane for about ¼ mile to a footpath sign on the left. Turn left, following the sign over a small bridge to take the path ahead over the field with Trent church spire directly ahead. The path crosses a stile beside the Rose and Crown pub. Turn right past the church on your left to return to your car.

SYDLING ST NICHOLAS

Length: 5 miles

Getting there: Sydling St Nicholas is 8 miles north-west of Dorchester. Turn off the A37, the Yeovil road, just north of Grimstone village, about 5 miles from Dorchester, and go under the railway bridge, following the sign for Sydling St Nicholas.

The road runs up the valley beside Sydling Water for just over 3 miles before entering the village.

Parking: Drive into the village and turn left just past the post office in front of a large tree,

following a wooden sign on the right for the church. The lane bears right at the top and there is ample parking on the left.

Map: OS Landranger 194. (GR 630993).

North of Dorchester chalk streams flowing south to meet the river Frome have carved deep valleys through the downs. One of the loveliest and least known is the valley of Sydling Water. The enchanting village of Sydling St Nicholas has the whole five miles of the valley to itself. Various branches of Sydling Water wind through the village and many of the houses, a pleasing mix of banded flint and stone, mellow brick, chalk and cob, often deep-thatched, are set behind colourful

FOOD and DRINK

The village pub, the Greyhound, is strongly recommended. Five real ales are offered. The restaurant is open from 12 noon to 2 pm and from 7 pm to 9 pm and the chef produces exciting menus. Telephone: 01300 341303.

gardens linked to the road by tiny bridges. The church dates back to the 13th century. Among several interesting features are the font, said to have been adzed from a Roman column, a 16th-century clock and an old hutch-type oak chest from the early 13th century. Nearby Court House incorporates part of a Tudor mansion, and in the High Street is the shaft and pedestal of a medieval wayside cross.

From the village the walk climbs high onto the downs to follow a ridge with glorious views for about 1¼ miles. From earliest times parts of these downs have been cultivated and the Celts have left the hillsides marked by traces of their settlements and terraced fields. The walk returns to the village through the lush watermeadows beside Sydling Water.

THE WALK

❶ From the parking area near the church and Court House, return down the lane to the road. Turn right along Dorchester Road and continue for about 100 yards. Just past the post office on the right, turn left over a wide grassy entry to cross a narrow bridge over Sydling Water. Go through a wooden gate and up the side of the meadow ahead with a hedge on the left. Continue through

The remains of the ancient market cross in Sydling St Nicholas.

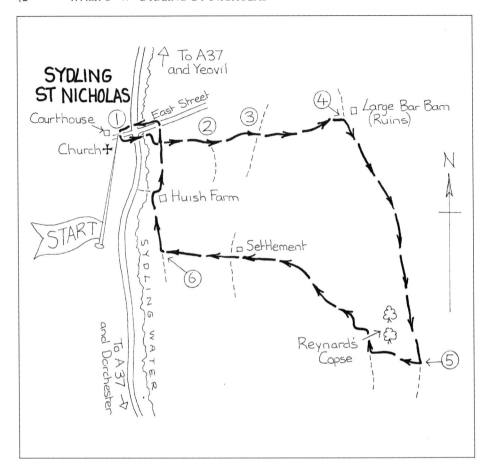

a gate which opens onto a white track leading uphill. The hillsides to the right are deeply scored with strip lynchets. Follow the track uphill until it turns right.

❷   Leave the main track here and go through the gate immediately ahead. An attractive grassy path curves across the hillside ahead to the next gate. After the gate, keep to the path as it curves a little right then passes a gate on the left to bring you to a gate on the top of the rise. Now you are rewarded by a splendid view of the valley of Sydling Water, the small village dwarfed by steep downland. Go through the gate and keep straight on with a hedge close on the left.

❸   Cross over the bridleway and continue ahead as the path dips then rises up a field following a line of posts. The top of the ridge is reached at a crosstrack running to the right of a hedge. Beyond the hedge is a small wood and the ruins of Large Bar Barn.

❹ Turn right with the hedge close on your left and follow the ridge. Keep on through the first gate. Ahead you will see two gates. Go through the small left-hand gate and continue with the hedge now close on your right to another gate. Go through and follow the path which now leads over the open hillside with the hedge some 30 yards away on your left. This brings you to another gate beside a wide gap in the hedge on the right which marks the end of our ridge walk.

❺ Turn right downhill with the hedge backed by a wire fence close on your right. Walk downhill, following a green path which shortly runs between double hedges to go through a gate. Keep straight on to go through another gate. Ahead you will see the curve of a white track. Follow it down into the valley to meet a crossing track. Turn right and pass Reynard's Copse on the hillside on your right. The path leads through a gate and curves left then right to continue ahead with a wire fence on the left. Follow the track as it bears left and climbs gently uphill through a gate. On the top of the rise embankments mark the site of an ancient settlement. The track becomes a concrete path and leads steeply down into the Sydling valley.

❻ The track turns right to pass Huish Farm and cross Sydling Water and meet a lane. Turn right signed for the Saw Mill and continue past the Mill and a pretty cottage up a narrow path which leads through a gate. Continue over the meadows beside Sydling Water through gates to join a road in the village. Walk past an attractive green on your left and turn left down East Street. Cross the road to walk up the lane to the church and your car.

CERNE ABBAS

Length: 6 miles

Getting there: Cerne Abbas is 5 miles north of Dorchester and signed off the A352. Approaching from the south, ignore the first turn on the right, signed for the village, and take the second lane on the right directly in front of the viewing area for the Cerne Abbas giant, signed for the picnic area. About 50 yards down the road turn left to the car park and picnic area.

Parking: In the picnic area as above.

Map: OS Landranger 194. (GR 664015).

Cerne Abbas is one of Dorset's treasures. It lies cradled in the downs, its narrow streets lined with a fascinating variety of houses: some built of stone and banded flint, others half-timbered and thatched, with here and there an elegant Georgian residence with curved bow windows. An abbey was founded here in AD 987 by Benedictine monks and today you can visit the romantic ruins. The church of St Mary the Virgin has 15th-century glass, an exceptional Jacobean pulpit and 14th-century wall paintings. Dominating the village from a westward-facing hillside is the famous Cerne Abbas giant, possibly dating from Romano-British times.

FOOD and DRINK

Cerne Abbas has three inns and some delightful tea shops.

The route of this walk climbs Giant Hill then follows a ridge above the Cerne valley giving splendid views. A quiet lane along a secret valley leads back to Cerne Abbas.

THE WALK

❶ From the picnic area turn left for a few yards, then turn right just before a bridge along a footpath running to the right of a stream. Continue to a bridge on the left. Cross the bridge and follow the path to Abbey Street. On the right is a row of timbered and jettied houses and opposite is the mill pond noisy with hungry ducks. Turn left towards Abbey Farm. To the right of the farm, gates lead to the Abbey ruins. Do not go through these gates, but turn right through the gates to the churchyard. Take the left-hand of the two paths ahead, go through another gate and keep ahead with a wall close on the left. At the entrance to the pottery bear half-right up the meadow to a stile leading to the wooded hillside. Cross, and follow the path uphill as it bears right then left through the trees to continue to the left of the fence round the giant. The very narrow path traces the steep hillside and curves round Giant Hill before becoming a wider green terrace leading a little more right, uphill. The path narrows through bushes to emerge on the open hillside again. Bear half-left towards a fence.

❷ Cross the stile over the fence and follow the path ahead which leads half-left to the right-hand edge of a copse and an iron-roofed barn. Keep straight on, passing the barn on your right. When the track bears right keep ahead to meet a road.

❸ Turn left beside the road for about ¼ mile. Our path leads from a small wooden gate on the left at the end of a wood. (A track leads right on the opposite side of the road.) Go through the gate and turn right to walk along the brow of the hillside to go through a gateway you will see ahead a little to your left. Continue along the hilltop with a fence on the left to go through a gate to a crosstrack.

❹ Turn left to follow this track along a ridge between two contrasting worlds: on one side the valley of the chalk stream and on the other the Vale of Blackmoor — Thomas Hardy's 'vale of little dairies'. After about ¼ mile go through a small iron gate on the left with a blue bridleway sign. Minterne Magna House is directly below you in the valley.

❺ Turn right for 100 yards then bear half-left downhill through a gate. Bear half-left again to go through a small wooden gate. Continue downhill through a gateway and

PLACES of INTEREST

The guest house and impressive porch to the **Abbot's lodging** have survived from the ruined abbey. They can be visited for a small fee. **Minterne Magna Gardens**, at their best in spring, are open from 28th March to 10th November, 10 am to 7 pm. There is an entrance fee.

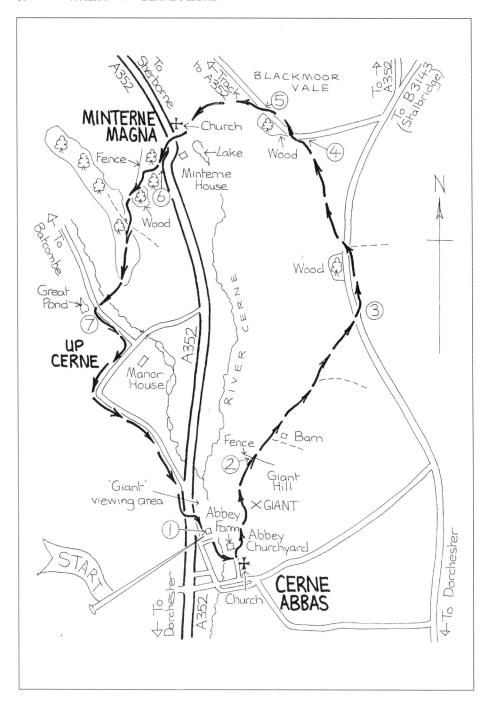

Abbey House, Cerne Abbas. The entrance to the Abbey ruins is on the right.

down the side of a field to go through another gate to a signpost. Bear right, signed 'Minterne', then turn left to cross a wooden footbridge and follow a lane to the A352 in Minterne Magna. Turn left past the gates to Minterne Magna Gardens and continue beside the road for about 200 yards.

❻ Turn right through a gate indicated with a blue bridleway sign and walk uphill through an avenue of trees. Go through the gate at the top and turn left to the open hillside. No clear path here but walk straight up the hill to a fence. Bear left with the fence on your right, go past a gate

and follow the path with a wood on your left. The path turns right and leads through a small wooden gate to a green crosstrack. Go over the track and follow a wide green way down into a quiet valley threaded by a tiny stream. The green way meets a lane in front of Great Pond.

❼ Turn left to follow the lane to Up Cerne with a splendid view of the manor house built around 1600. At the T-junction turn right past the manor on the left and follow the lane for a little under a mile to meet the A352. Turn right past the Giant viewing area and descend the lane to the car park and picnic area.

PUDDLETOWN

Length: 5 miles

Getting there: Puddletown is a large village on the A35 about 6 miles east of Dorchester. Approaching from Dorchester, drive into the village, pass the first set of traffic lights, and turn left down Mill Street. Take the first turning on the right to the church which is on the right. Approaching from the east, pass the first set of traffic lights and turn almost immediately sharp right into Mill Street.

Parking: On the left of the road, opposite the church.

Map: OS Landranger 194. (GR 758945).

Puddletown is the 'Weatherbury' of Thomas Hardy's novel *Far from the Madding Crowd*. It is a village with a unique character. Cob and thatch mingle happily with uniform houses erected in mock Gothic style by the squire, John Brymer, in 1864. The glory of the village is its mainly 15th-century church, famous for its musicians' gallery, the alabaster figures in the Martyn chapel and the 17th-century woodwork.

Starting from the church, the walk climbs out of the Puddle valley to descend into the valley of the Frome through the curving downland, quiet valleys and coppiced woods immortalised by Thomas Hardy. The return route crosses attractive heathland and follows part of the Rhododendron Drive, famous for its blaze of colour in early summer.

THE WALK

❶ With Puddletown church on your left, turn left along a narrow path running between the church tower and the graveyard to the main road. Cross, and turn left along the pavement to continue though the village. Just after the Weatherbury Garage turn right up a track with a blue arrow bridleway sign. The lane climbs between high banks out of the Puddle valley then dips into another valley as quiet and remote as it must have been in Hardy's day. Go through a gate, past farm buildings on the left, and continue up the lane to walk through Ilsington Wood, a good example of managed woodland with coppiced hazels and standard oaks. Just past a pond on the right the path continues beside the woods with meadows rising on the left. Leave the woods through an iron gate and continue beside a meadow. The path curves a little left then rises gently to meet a crosstrack.

❷ Go over the crosstrack to a gate in the wire fence a little to your right. Pause here

to enjoy a splendid view over the rich Frome valley – Hardy's 'vale of great dairies'. Here the heroine of *Tess of the d'Urbervilles* spent her happiest days. Go through the gate and although the path is faint navigation presents no problems. Just continue straight ahead over the grass and when you see an avenue of oak trees walk between the trees downhill to go through a gate to a lane. Turn right and follow the lane for about ½ mile.

❸ When the lane ahead bends to pass to the left of some cottages look for a path on the right marked with a blue arrow bridleway sign. Turn right along this path through oak woodland, leaving the cottages on your left. Just past the cottages, bear right to some wooden barriers at the approach to Puddletown Forest. Two possible paths lead ahead at this point. Take the right-hand path along the edge of the wood leading between tall pines on the left and hazels and oaks on the right. Gradually the path rises through more open areas. The open heathland looks as wild as the 'Egdon' of Hardy's *The Return of the Native*.

Puddletown church. In Thomas Hardy's novel Far from the Madding Crowd *Sergeant Troy spent an unhappy night i the porch.*

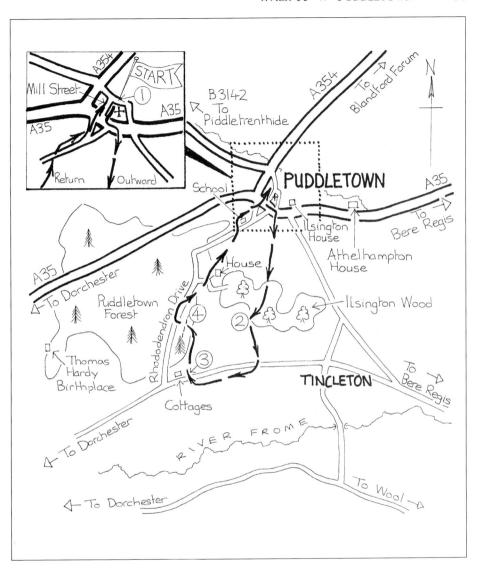

Keep to the main path as it bears left over a crosstrack to descend to a road, Rhododendron Drive. Turn right to follow the road for about 150 yards between the high walls of rhododendrons which give the road its name.

❹ Turn right, following the bridleway sign along a path leading over heath dotted with gorse, silver birches and pines to a gate into a meadow. Go through the gate, turn left to walk up the meadow and go through another gate. Continue straight over the field ahead (a path may not be visible) to leave the field by a small iron gate. (Ignore the larger gate in front of a brick building about 50 yards to your right.) Cross straight over the farm track to take a narrow path through the woods directly ahead. Pass a house on the right to leave the woods through a small wooden gate. There may be no clear path but go through the gate and follow the poles supporting power lines over two fields to a gate in the top right-hand corner of the second field. Continue to a road, cross over and take the footpath ahead. Climb the stile and continue with a hedge on your left. Puddletown is tucked comfortably in the valley on your right. The path bears left through a gate then bears right to resume its northerly heading past the school beside a wire fence. When you see a stile ahead, do not cross, but follow the path as it turns right, still beside the wire fence, to bring you to the school gates. Past the gates turn left to follow a raised footpath beside Coombe Road which leads to the A35. Cross and follow Mill Street, turning right for the church and your car.

WALK 11

MORETON

Length: 5½ miles

Getting there: Moreton lies in the Frome valley between Dorchester and Wareham. From the A35 (Bere Regis-Dorchester) turn for Affpuddle along the B3390. Follow the signs for Moreton, turning left off the B3390 for the village. From the A352 (Wareham-Dorchester) turn for Moreton along the B3390 and shortly after the level crossing turn right for the village.

Parking: Follow the sign 'To the Church'. Continue down the lane past the post office and park on the left. The river is directly ahead.

Map: OS Landranger 194. (GR 805884).

Settled comfortably in fertile meadows beside the river Frome, Moreton is a tiny village of mostly brick or cob cottages, deeply thatched with diamond-paned windows. But this secluded little village possesses one of the most wonderful churches in Dorset. The pale blue and white apsidal chancel is lit by a glorious sequence of engraved glass windows by Lawrence Whistler. And in the cemetery you will find the grave of Lawrence of Arabia.

An easy walk through pine woods leads to T. E. Lawrence's cottage at Clouds Hill before passing Thomas Hardy's 'Alderworth', the home of Clym and Eustacia in his novel *The Return of the Native*. Paths through beautiful oak woods lead back to Moreton.

THE WALK

❶ Cross the narrow footbridge over the river Frome and keep ahead up the track. Ignore two footpath signs on the left. Shortly after, a track joins on the right. Turn right to follow this track which runs between meadows dotted with oaks. The track turns left. When another track joins on the right, bear left again following the yellow arrow footpath sign.

❷ When the track divides, take the right-hand track which begins to climb gently.

❸ Leave the wider track along the next track on the right - you will see a yellow footpath sign on a tree on the right. This climbs steeply to the top of the ridge from where you can look back over pinewoods to the valley of the Frome. Go through the

Crossing the river Frome at Moreton.

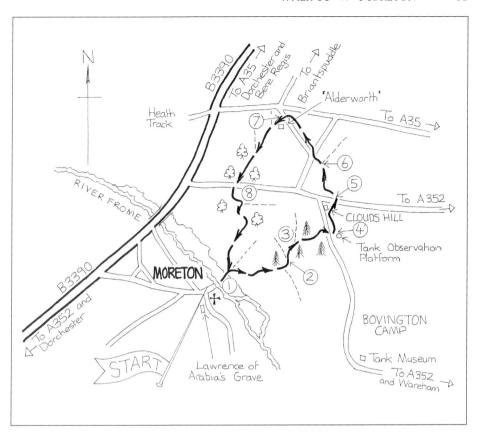

wooden gate in front of a tank training area – the Royal Armoured Corps centre is at Bovington Camp nearby. Follow the footpath signs which lead left then round to the left of the training area to the road which runs south to Bovington Camp and Wool. Cross the road to the tank observation area. An information board illustrates the various models you will see practising manoeuvres.

❹ Just to the left of the wooden posts in front of the observation area a narrow path runs parallel with the road, separated from it by a belt of bushes and trees. Turn left

and follow this path beside a wire fence. Turn right as signs direct, keeping the wire fence close on the right. After a few yards the path bears a little left and climbs before dropping to meet a road.

❺ Turn left and walk along the grass verge beside the road for a few yards to the junction with the road to Bovington. Lawrence of Arabia's cottage, Clouds Hill, is a few yards down the road on the left. The tiny brick and tiled cottage, which he bought in 1923 as a retreat when serving as aircraftsman Ross at Bovington Camp has been preserved exactly as he left it. Return

grass verge – for about ½ mile.

❼ Turn left along a footpath to walk to the right of a row of cottages, Thomas Hardy's 'Alderworth'. Follow a path into a wood and bear left when you meet a better defined track. Keep ahead over a crosstrack and follow the blue signs to continue through Oakers Wood. The path leads to a road. Cross and take the green path ahead heading uphill with fields on the right. The path leads into oak woods. Continue for about 150 yards.

❽ Look carefully for a path on the right. On a tree some yards down the path you will see a Jubilee Trail sign, a small white fir tree on a disc. Turn right and after about 50 yards turn left, still following the Jubilee Trail signs. The narrow path leaves the trees by a stile. Cross a wooden footbridge and walk straight across the field ahead. Continue to cross more fields and stiles then bear left as the signs direct to walk round a field with a wire fence close on the left. Cross the stile on the left to rejoin our outward bound route a few yards from the river. Turn right to return over the footbridge to Moreton and your car.

to the junction, cross straight over the road and take the bridleway directly ahead (indicated with a blue arrow). After a few yards bear left as the arrow directs then follow the signs across the heath. Go through a gate and turn left. Bear left again to continue along a rutted track.

❻ When the rutted track begins to curve right, keep straight on with a wire fence close on your left. After about 100 yards the path brings you to a road junction. Cross over and keep ahead along the road signed for Briantspuddle – there is a wide

MILTON ABBAS

Length: 7 miles

Getting there: Milton Abbas is 3 miles off the A354 Puddletown to Blandford Road. Follow the signs to Milton Abbas from Milborne St Andrew or	Winterborne Whitechurch. **Parking:** Drive downhill into the village where there is roadside parking.	**Map:** OS Landranger 194. (GR 807018).

No calendar depicting Dorset villages would be complete without a picture of Milton Abbas. Tucked firmly in a wooded cleft in the chalk downs is a single street lined with identical thatched-roofed and whitewashed cob cottages set behind carefully manicured lawns. Beyond them colourful gardens mount the steep hillside.

The whole village was planned in the 18th century by 'Capability' Brown at the request of Lord Damer, Earl of Dorchester, who, having acquired Milton Abbey, objected to the neighbouring town of Middleton. He destroyed Middleton and removed the inhabitants to his new village, Milton Abbas. Today the village is picture-postcard pretty but in the 18th century the double cottages were overcrowded and can have been poor compensation for the evicted tenants of the flourishing market town!

The setting of this unique village and the abbey in the Delcombe Valley is idyllic and this walk reveals its beauty to the full. After visiting the abbey, woodland paths follow the valley to the remote village of Hilton sheltering beneath one of Thomas

Hardy's Wessex heights, Bulbarrow. The route then climbs Coombe Hill, a magnificent viewpoint, before returning along pleasant lanes.

THE WALK

❶ Walk down the village street, leaving the church on your left and the almshouses on your right. At the road junction turn right, signed 'Milton Abbey'. After about 50 yards bear left in front of a thatched cottage to follow a footpath with the lake on the left to Milton Abbey. The lake and surrounding lawns replaced the destroyed town. Walk up to a crosspath at the approach to the south front of Milton Abbey. We turn right here but if you wish to visit the abbey keep ahead to the west door. Built of golden Ham Hill stone, the

Milton Abbey.

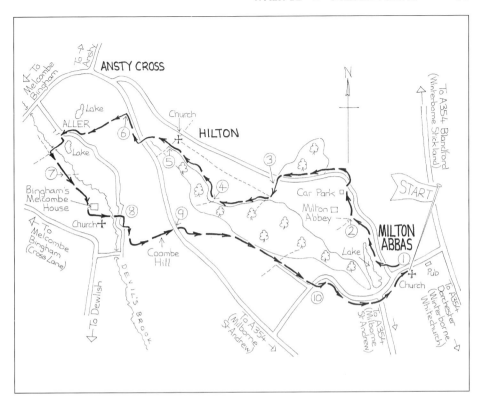

abbey dates from the 14th and 15th centuries and was part of a Benedictine monastery until the Dissolution in 1539. Lord Damer's mock Gothic mansion, now a school, stands nearby.

❷ Turn right and follow the path up to the abbey car park and tea rooms. Follow the 'Exit' signs to a road and turn left. Pass the school gates and playing fields on the left and continue uphill for about ½ mile past a wood on the right.

❸ Turn left along an avenue of fine beech trees to a crosspath at the edge of woods and turn right. (Not the valley path marked on the OS map. Our path is

unmarked but is a public right of way.) When the path forks keep ahead, right-hand path, along the edge of the woods.

❹ When the main track turns left, keep ahead along a narrow path, still following the edge of the woods with Hilton village in the valley on your right, to a crosspath.

❺ Keep straight ahead. The path turns

PLACES of INTEREST

Milton Abbey Church is open throughout the year. During Easter and the summer holidays a fee is charged but this includes a visit to the mansion.

left uphill through a wooden gate to a meadow. Cross over the field to go through a gate to a lane. Turn right and continue for about ¼ mile.

❻ Turn left, signed 'Bridleway', to walk down into the valley of the Devil's Brook. A gate leads you to a lane in Aller. Keep ahead between two thatched cottages and after about 100 yards turn left along a stony track. A few yards further turn left through two gates with farm buildings on the right. After the second gate turn right to walk down the field to cross a narrow concrete bridge. Walk ahead for a few yards then bear left along a grassy path to go through a gate and along the edge of a field with the stream on the left. Step over a wire to continue ahead and follow the path downhill through a newly planted area.

❼ The path divides in front of a post with footpath signs. Take the right-hand path which follows the stream then turns left through a gate and crosses to a wide green avenue. Turn right to walk past the walled gardens of Elizabethan Bingham's Melcombe House to a track. Bear left past the main entrance to the house on the left and the little church and old school on the right. Cross the bridge over Devil's Brook, turn right and walk up to a lane.

❽ Bear right for about 50 yards then turn left along the footpath for Coombe Hill. Go through the gate at the foot of the hill and follow the path as it curves right then left to bring you to the top with a magnificent view as your reward. Continue round the top of the coombe and go through a gate to a road.

❾ Turn right for about 80 yards then turn left along a good track. Keep to this attractive way for about a mile over a crosstrack to a lane at a T-junction.

❿ Turn left and follow the lane as it bends right to return to the main road by Milton Abbey lake. Keep straight ahead for Milton Abbas.

OKEFORD FITZPAINE

Length: 6 miles

Getting there: Okeford Fitzpaine is a small village 2 miles off the A357 between Sturminster Newton and Blandford Forum. Drive into Shillingstone village and take the turning (Poplar Road) for Okeford Fitzpaine opposite the church. The road bends left to pass the church in Okeford Fitzpaine. Just past the church leave the road and turn left up the narrow lane marked with a no through road sign. This leads to the village hall.

Parking: Opposite the village hall there is a large parking area. There is short time parking here for visitors to the village by permission of the parish council.

Map: OS Landranger 194. (GR 807108).

Okeford Fitzpaine is a charming village in the southern Blackmoor Vale at the foot of a steep bluff of the North Dorset downs. In *Highways and Byways in Dorset*, written almost a hundred years ago, the historian Frederick Treves described Okeford Fitzpaine as being 'a part of the Dorset of old days'. That description is still true today. From the church on the hill you look down on deep-thatched houses, many half-timbered, set among green lawns and gardens. Opposite the 17th-century village

FOOD and DRINK

The Royal Oak in the centre of Okeford Fitzpaine is strongly recommended for excellent food and ales. Telephone: 01258 860308. In nearby Shillingstone you will find The Willows, a delightful tea room serving meals throughout the day. The tea room is beside the Blandford road – look for the sign, a large teapot. Telephone: 01258 861167.

stores stands the stone base of a medieval cross. And the village still has its own fire engine dated 1895, complete with helmet

This varied walk includes panoramic views over the Blackmoor Vale, quiet woodland paths and part of the historic Wessex Ridgeway. The return route passes

through Ringmoor where you can see traces of an ancient settlement.

THE WALK

❶ Leave the front of the village hall on your right and turn right up a footpath, passing some garages on your left. The path rises to a crosstrack. Turn left and continue along the wide track as it bears right to climb Okeford Hill. Keep straight ahead through an iron gate (ignore the gate on the left) which opens onto the grassy hillside. Continue ahead leaving a large mound enclosed within a wire fence on your right. Go through a gate – a road is a few yards away on your right – and follow the narrow path as it leads up the hill ahead through two small gates. At the top the path continues along the crest of the

The view over the Stour valley from Okeford Hill.

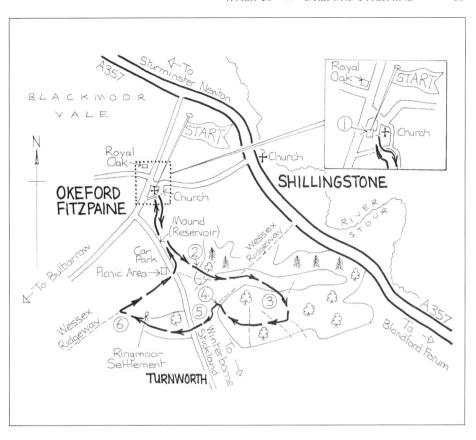

hill towards a line of trees on the skyline.

❷ Go through a gate to walk through a beech wood to a crosstrack. Cross over and keep ahead to meet a wide, firm track – the Wessex Ridgeway. Bear left along this ancient highway dating back four thousand years when it was used by Bronze Age traders. After about ¼ mile turn right along another ridgeway which crosses open fields towards pine woods. Keep straight ahead over a crosstrack to enter the woods.

❸ Continue to a crosstrack. Bear half-right here to walk through mixed woods of

beech, hazel and oak. After about ¼ mile you come to another crosstrack by a concrete ramp. Turn right to follow the gravel track which descends slightly to a junction of several paths. Continue along the gravel track which bears a little left then descends over a crosstrack. Keep ahead as the path leads uphill to leave the woods.

❹ Leave the track as it turns right, and bear left with the woods on your left. The field on your right is dotted with Bronze Age burial mounds. The path leads between gateposts to the top of Turnworth

Down. Bear left for a few yards then bear right to resume your original heading downhill over the grass with a hedge of tall trees on your left. Go through a gate and continue down the steep hillside to a wooden gate in the valley opening onto the Turnworth-Okeford Fitzpaine road.

❺   Cross the road to go through the opposite gate by the National Trust sign for Ringmoor and Turnworth Down. Behind the sign a wooden finger post indicates the path up the hill a little to your left. When the path divides keep to the right-hand path which climbs steadily through beautiful woods of mature oaks, beeches and coppiced hazels. The path winds across a more open grassy area, rich in wild flowers and a haven in high summer for butterflies. Already you will notice irregular hummocks and embankment marking the roads and hut platforms of Ringmoor ancient settlement. As the path

crosses the grass at the top of the down these become more prominent and there is the raised outline of a circular henge monument about 30 yards from the path on the right. Go through a gate to pass Ringmoor Pond on your left and another gate brings you to the Wessex Ridgeway once more.

❻   Turn right to follow the Ridgeway and enjoy breathtaking views over the Blackmoor Vale towards Shaftesbury and Cranborne Chase. Pass Okeford Hill car park and picnic area to meet a lane. Turn left down the lane and walk downhill towards Okeford Fitzpaine which you will see in the valley below. Just before the prominent mound you passed outward bound, turn right through a gate to rejoin your earlier route to the right of the mound. Retrace your steps down to the parking area close to the church and the village hall.

IWERNE COURTNEY

Length: 3½ miles

Getting there: Iwerne Courtney (also called Shroton) lies just west of the A350 about 5 miles north of Blandford Forum. From Blandford Forum follow the signs for Warminster and Shaftesbury. Turn left for Iwerne Courtney. The road turns right to pass the church which is on the left.

Parking: There is a large parking area opposite the church.

Map: OS Landranger 194. (GR 859125).

Iwerne Courtney is beautifully set in a wide green valley sheltered by the steep slopes of Hambledon Hill. The village is an attractive mix of old and new – stone-built thatched cottages and neat Georgian houses which blend happily with more modern developments. The church has a 14th-century nave and tower and in front of the Freke chapel is a delicately carved 17th-century screen.

The charm of this walk is the magnificent view you will enjoy from the embankments of the Iron Age fort on the top of Hambledon Hill. This is gained with very little effort as the climb is easy and gradual. But take care if the ground is

FOOD and DRINK

The Cricketers serves bar snacks and full meals in the restaurant and has a wide range of real ales. Telephone: 01258 860421.

wet as the chalk can be slippery.

THE WALK

❶ With the parking area on your right walk a few yards up the village street and turn left down Fairfield Road. You pass a massive thatched barn on your left. The lane bears round to the right towards the cricket pitch. Just before the pavilion look for a stile and bridleway sign on the left. Cross the stile and, leaving the cricket pitch on your right, walk half-left diagonally up the hill towards a stone wall.

❷ Go through a metal gate and a few yards further on turn right uphill to continue through another metal gate. Already there are wide views over the Iwerne valley to the slopes of Cranborne Chase. And as you gain more height you will see ahead the great earth embankments of Hambledon Iron Age hill fort. The path leads to a grassy crosstrack marked by a prominent trig point. Our way is to the right but before you turn look over the gate opposite the trig point. The humps and bumps in the field beyond the gate mark the site of a Neolithic causewayed camp which was probably inhabited around 2790 BC. To the left beyond the camp rise the hills of the North

A massive thatched barn at Iwerne Courtney.

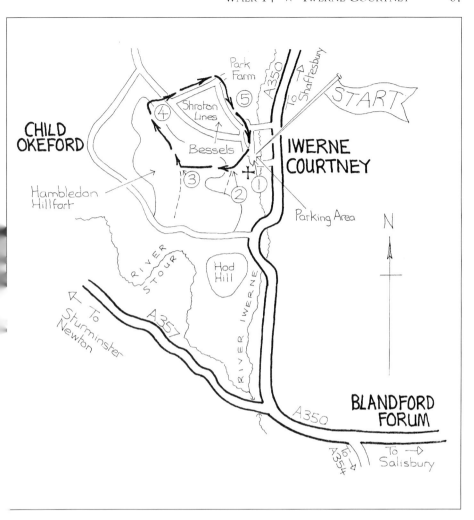

Dorset downs with the Vale of Blackmoor at their foot.

3 Turn right to walk down the grassy track to a gate opening onto Hambledon Hill beside the fort embankments. A notice board states that this chalk downland grazed by sheep is rich in flowers including early gentians and meadow saxifrage. Butterflies include the rare

Adonis Blue. Continue along the path which traces the side of Hambledon Hill. General Wolfe trained his soldiers on these steep slopes to prepare them to scale the Heights of Abraham and capture Quebec. On the right the embankments of the Iron Age fort rise equally steeply but they failed to protect the Celtic inhabitants against the Roman general Vespasian who led the Second Augusta Legion against them in

AD 43. Another battle took place in 1645 when a number of local men, weary of the Civil War between Royalists and Parliamentarians, gathered here and defied Cromwell. They were routed by his trained troops. Cromwell ordered the survivors to be locked in Iwerne Courtney church for the night and to be set free in the morning.

Keep to the good path as it descends a little with a fence close on the right. The path starts to drop more steeply then turns round to the right, bearing left as it reaches the foot of the hill and a wooden gate. Go through the gate and keep ahead beside a field to a crosstrack.

❹ Ignore the stile opposite and turn right along the crosstrack. This leads to a lane at Shroton Lines. Turn right for a few yards then bear left along the lane for Bessels, leaving a cottage on your right. Keep to the lane as it turns right past the track to Park Farm. Continue along the lane past Bessels, an attractive hamlet. Just past the last house in the hamlet look for a footpath sign on the left at the foot of a flight of stone steps. Turn left up the steps and cross the stile at the top. There is no clear path at this point but you will see the houses of Iwerne Courtney across the fields ahead.

❺ From the stile bear half-right diagonally over the field, leaving a line of power cables on your left. Go through a gap in a fence to the right of the cables then bear a little left to go through two gates to a lane in the village. Follow the lane as it turns right past attractive houses to a crossroads. Keep straight ahead down Main Street past the Cricketers pub and the village green to your car on the left opposite the church.

WINTERBORNE ZELSTON

Length: 4 miles

Getting there: Winterborne Zelston lies just north of the A31 between Bere Regis and Wimborne Minster. Approaching from the east you will see the Botany Bay Inn on the left overlooking the main street in Winterborne Zelston on the other side of the A31.

Parking: As parking in the village is limited and the Botany Bay serves excellent food all day I would advise you to enjoy a visit to the inn and leave your car in its car park. The landlord is happy for patrons to leave their cars while they walk. If you are parking anywhere else in the village, please do so with

care and consideration for residents, and bear in mind that its narrow roads are easily obstructed.

Maps: OS Landranger 194 and 195 (the walk starts and ends on 195, with its middle section shown on 194). (GR 899974).

Although so close to a busy road, Winterborne Zelston is Dorset at its most appealing – serene and timeless. The main street leads downhill past mostly thatched and whitewashed houses to lose itself in lawns beside the little Winterborne stream. Willows trail long branches in the water and in summer the banks are bright with flowers. Beside the pond stands the base of a Saxon preaching cross. Close by an irresistibly-placed seat will tempt you to linger and watch the antics of the ducks! This is an ideal outing for all the family. Meadow paths lead beside the stream to visit two more hamlets with 'Winterborne' in their names (there are fifteen in all). At Winterborne Tomson you will discover one of Dorset's gems, a tiny, perfectly preserved, early 12th-cen-

tury church furnished in oak during the 18th century with high-sided box pews, a singing gallery, a simple screen, pulpit and tester now all aged to a delicate silver-grey. The manor house at Winterborne Anderson (usually referred to as just Anderson) was built in 1622 and is a splendid example of Jacobean architecture. The return route follows the course of a Roman road, then runs through woods full of flowers in season before descending to Winterborne Zelston down a quiet lane.

THE WALK

❶ From the Botany Bay inn car park cross the A31 and walk down the village street. At the foot of the street turn right. The base of the Saxon preaching cross is on your left with the Winterborne stream

The 12th-century church at Winterborne Tomson restored by money resulting from the sale of Thomas Hardy manuscripts.

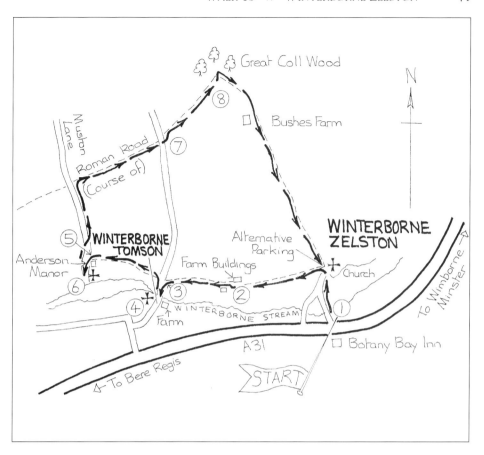

widening round an island beyond. Bear left over a small bridge past the church. Walk up the lane and turn left for the village hall, following the footpath sign for Winterborne Kingston. Climb the stile ahead and follow the path with the stream running through the fields on your left. Climb the next stile and continue towards some farm buildings.

❷ Go through the gate and continue for a few yards past the first of the farm buildings. Do not go through the metal gate immediately ahead but turn right to walk between the buildings. Past the buildings, turn left along an asphalt lane, leaving a house on your left. The pretty lane fringed with small trees leads to a crosstrack.

❸ Turn left to walk past the farm at Winterborne Tomson, an impressive 17th-century house with massive gables and tall clustered chimneys. Go through the farmyard gate to see Winterborne Tomson church on the right. This tiny church stands isolated in the meadows. Much loved by Thomas Hardy, the church was rescued from dereliction and restored with great care by the architect A.R. Powys in the 1920s using the proceeds of a sale of Thomas Hardy's manuscripts and a donation from Lord Esher.

❹ Retrace your steps past the farm to where you turned left for Winterborne Tomson. Turn left over the stile and cross the field ahead. Look for a stile in the hedge a little to your right. Cross and continue ahead to meet a crossing lane, Muston Lane.

❺ Turn left to follow the lane to the church. From the churchyard you can glimpse the heavy gables and stone-mullioned windows of Anderson Manor. Built of rich red brick faced with limestone the house has remained almost unaltered for three and a half centuries. During the Second World War the manor was requisitioned as the Headquarters of the Special Operations Small Raiding Force. The Force carried out a series of highly successful raids on German-occupied territory including a canoe raid on the

shipping in the river Gironde at Bordeaux, the story behind *The Cockleshell Heroes.*

❻ Retrace your steps and continue ahead up Muston Lane for just over ¼ mile. Look carefully for gaps in the hedge on either side of the lane. There are bridleway blue arrow signs marking a crosstrack but these may be obscured. Leave Muston Lane and turn right beside a field with a hedge on your right. The path follows the course of a Roman road and leads through gates to a lane.

❼ Turn left for only a few yards then turn right through a gate leading to an attractive path through a fringe of woodland. Go through the next gate and keep to the woodland path as it bears left to the corner of Great Coll Wood.

❽ Turn right to go through a gate into a field. Down the field a little to your right you will see Bushes Farm. Walk down the field to continue along a track, leaving the farm buildings on your right. Follow the lane ahead to Winterborne Zelston.

ASHMORE

Length: 4 miles

Getting There: Ashmore is a small village in north-east Dorset, about 4 miles south-east of Shaftesbury. Approaching from Shaftesbury, head south on the A350 and turn

left in Fontmell Magna for Ashmore. The best approach from the south is to take the A350 north from Blandford Forum, turning right in Fontmell Magna for Ashmore.

Parking: There is room to park by the large pond in Ashmore, opposite the war memorial.

Map: OS Landranger 184. (GR 913178).

Ashmore is off the beaten track but well worth finding. A rare survival of a Saxon hilltop settlement, it is the highest village in Dorset, commanding wonderful views over the rolling countryside of Cranborne Chase as far as Salisbury Plain and south and east over Hampshire to the Channel coast. Dark-thatched houses built of green- gold stone and flint cluster around an embanked pond which is home for a noisy tribe of mallard and muscovy ducks. Even in the hottest summer their playground never dries up! Every year, at Midsummer, the villagers pay tribute to their pond in an ancient ceremony called 'Filly Loo' when Morris men dance on the shore to music

FOOD and DRINK

Good, home-cooked food is served all day at the Crown pub in Fontmell Magna, about 4 miles from Ashmore. Telephone: 01747 811441.

provided by a band on a platform in the water.

The great forests that once covered the chalk downlands of Cranborne Chase have largely disappeared but it is still possible to find remote glens and mysterious woodlands. This walk around Ashmore explores one of these areas. The only sounds you will hear as you tread these quiet woodland ways will be the harsh cry of pheasants and perhaps the brushing of deer through the undergrowth.

THE WALK

❶ With the pond on your left and the war memorial on your right walk up the road past the church. After about 50 yards turn left down Halfpenny Lane, following the bridleway sign. Follow the lane as it runs high over the downs giving fine views over the undulating countryside of Cranborne Chase. Keep straight ahead down the main track as it runs through lightly wooded areas towards the dark line of Ashmoor Wood. The entrance to the wood is marked by some splendid oaks and beeches.

❷ Keep straight ahead over the crosstrack into Ashmoor Wood. Although at this point pine trees predominate, the woods are noted for their flowers: primroses, violets and bluebells early in the year, to be followed by white anemones and tall stands of foxgloves. Continue for about ¼ mile.

❸ When you come to a junction of paths, take the second path on the left, indicated by a blue arrow bridleway sign on a post. Follow this path for about another ¼ mile to the edge of the wood to meet a crosstrack.

❹ Turn left along an attractive path with woods fringed with young beeches, hollies and hazels on your left and glimpses of open countryside through the hedge on your right. The path descends into a valley to a crosstrack.

❺ Our path is not immediately obvious at this point. Turn right for a few yards to a metal gate. Do not go through the gate but turn left up a path you will now see leading steeply uphill. The path bears a little left and climbs more gently through old woods full of snowdrops in early spring. The way then leaves the woods and continues between a fringe of trees with fields beyond to rise to meet a crosstrack.

❻ Again our path is not immediately obvious. Turn right for just a few yards towards a gate. Do not go through the gate but turn left before it along a hedged path. After about ¼ mile look for two iron gates either side of the path. At this point the path is crossed by the line of the Roman road which ran from Hamworthy on Poole Harbour via Badbury Rings (Roman Vindocladia) to Bath. If you look over the field on the right you will see the darker green furrows marking the route. Keep to the path as it drops steeply into a shallow green valley, Tollard Green Bottom, the boundary between Dorset and Wiltshire. The path turns left along the valley and

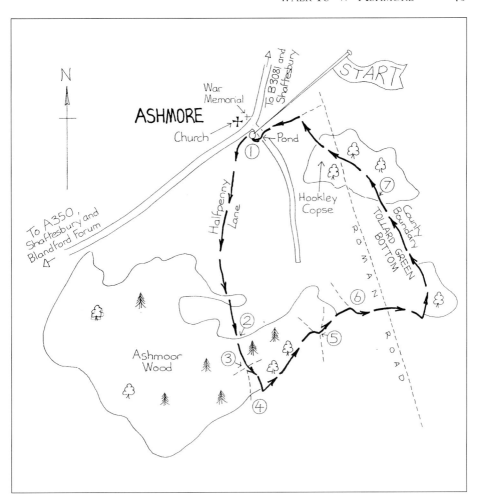

enters old oak and beech woods. After running through a more open area with fields either side the path enters another old wood. Keep straight on past a path on the right for about 50 yards.

❼ At this point the path divides. Take the right-hand path, an attractive grassy way leading a little uphill through Hookley Copse. Keep to the path as the woods on the left give way to parkland with the rooftops of Ashmore showing above the rise beyond. Cross a stile and continue straight on to cross another stile and follow a winding woodland path to a crosspath. Turn left to cross a stile and follow a broad grassy way marked by a finger post until you go through a gate and meet a road in Ashmore. Turn right to walk back to the pond and your car.

WORTH MATRAVERS

Length: 4½ miles

Getting there: Head south from Wareham along the A351. Follow signs for Corfe Castle and after driving through the village bear right along the B3069 for Kingston. In Kingston	keep to the B3069 as it turns left for Swanage. After about a mile turn right for Worth Matravers. **Parking:** In just over a mile, as you approach the village, there	is a large car park on the right. **Map:** OS Landranger 195. (GR 973774).

The Isle of Purbeck is a distinct and very beautiful part of Dorset, divided from the rest of the county by a ridge of chalk downland dominated by the romantic ruins of Corfe Castle. Beyond the chalk are limestone hills and at their most southerly point great walls of rock honeycombed

with former quarries confront the sea close to St Aldhelm's Head. Not far from the Head, overlooking a steep-sided ravine leading down to the sea and the quarries at Winspit, lies one of the most picturesque of all the Purbeck villages, Worth Matravers. Narrow streets lined with houses built and

FOOD and DRINK

The Square and Compass is a little whitewashed pub retaining the timeless atmosphere of bygone days. A narrow stone-flagged passage leads to a serving hatch and you can enjoy drinks and snacks in one of the cosy, low-beamed rooms or on the terrace overlooking the valley. Telephone: 01929 439229. Full meals are served at the Worth Cafe and Craft Centre opposite the pub, open all week except Tuesday.

houses are alike, some have tiny windows, deep-set beneath an irregular roofline, others have rounded bows only a foot or so above the stone-flagged pavement.

This walk traces the steps of the quarrymen down the Winspit valley, then climbs to the clifftop to follow the coast path to St Aldhelm's Head, offering magnificent views before returning over the downs.

THE WALK

roofed with local dove-grey stone cluster around a 12th-century church. No two

❶ From the car park entrance turn right down the lane into the village. Pass the

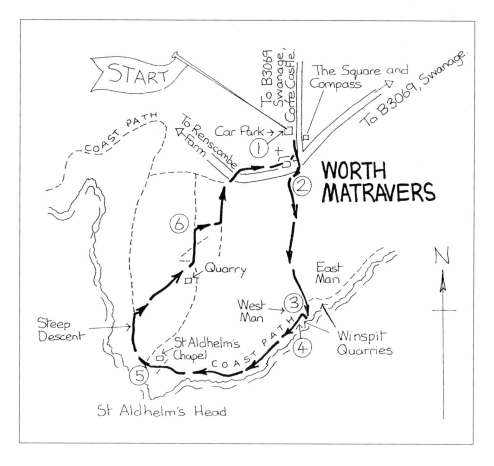

Winspit quarry, near Worth Matravers.

Square and Compass on the left and turn right at the T-junction. Bear left downhill to leave the village pond on your right and follow the sign for Winspit. Bear right past a small woodland garden and when the road divides turn left down a lane marked with a 'no through road' sign. At the end of the lane keep straight on over a stile along an embanked footpath. Cross the next stile to emerge on the open hillside and look south to the sea framed by downs scored by medieval strip lynchets.

❷ Follow the path as it curves round the hillside and descends into the valley. Cross the stile and continue past a joining track on the right. Keep to the main track as it descends almost to sea level. You pass a sign for the Coast Path on the right. Close to

the sea, looking like cave dwellings for giants, stand the huge Winspit quarries. Until 1950 valuable Purbeck limestone was tunnelled out of the cliffs to be lowered onto barges and transported to Swanage. The industry boomed in the 18th century when stone was needed to rebuild London after the Great Fire.

PLACES of INTEREST

Corfe Castle is one of the most impressive ruins in England. Open from 10 am to 5.30 pm during March to October and from 11 am to 3.30 pm during November to February. Telephone: 01929 481294. A fascinating audio-visual account of the siege can be enjoyed in the National Trust centre in Corfe Castle car park. The **Swanage Steam Railway** runs to Corfe Castle. For details telephone: 01929 424276.

❸ Retrace your steps for a few yards to the Coast Path sign, now on your left. Turn left to climb round the edge of one of the quarries to the clifftop and enjoy a stunning view eastwards to Anvil Point. The cottage tucked among the trees in the Winspit valley was once the home of Jeremiah Bower, always known as Billy Winspit. He was the last man to quarry stone here, working from the age of eleven until just short of his 80th birthday.

❹ Follow the clifftop path which climbs towards St Aldhelm's Head. Bear left when the path divides to a crosspath. Go over and keep ahead uphill. Below, on the left, the ruined buildings are the bombed remains of a wartime Telecommunications Research Department where experimental work on radar was carried out. Pass the Coastguard Station to the tiny Norman chapel dedicated to St Aldhelm, 8th-century bishop of Sherborne. It is a fascinating building, square and low, with a single pier supporting the stone-vaulted roof.

❺ Return to the cliff path and continue round the headland to enjoy a wonderful view over the long line of undulating cliffs which run west to Weymouth Bay and Portland. You come to a steep cleft at the seaward end of a shallow valley. Descend the steps and at the foot turn right over a stile and follow the path which leads up the valley past a working quarry on the right. Just past the quarry look for a stile on your right. Cross the stile to the track leading to the quarry and bear left uphill past a track on the left to meet a crosstrack. Bear left and continue for about ¼ mile.

❻ Look for a barn on the right and a stone marking a bridleway, 'Worth ¼'. Turn right to leave the barn on your left. Continue with a hedge on your left to a crosstrack. Turn left, signed for Worth, and keep ahead to meet a road. Turn right to walk to the village. Pass the pond on your right and turn left to return to the car park.

WITCHAMPTON

Length: 3 or 6 miles

Getting there: Witchampton is 4 miles north of Wimborne Minster and reached via the B3078. From Wimborne Minster the road is signed 'Cranborne'. It crosses the river Allen then follows the river valley to Stanbridge. About a mile further turn left signed	'Witchampton 1½ miles'. **Parking:** The road crosses the Allen to enter the village and turns right past the old mill. Continue past a lane on the left, round a bend, and as the roads bends right once more turn left up a steep entry signed	'mini recycling centre' in front of a school sign. This leads up past the church on the right to a large parking area behind the village hall. **Map:** OS Landranger 195. (GR 988064).

Witchampton is as beguiling as its name suggests. Set in gentle pastoral countryside beside the river Allen, the village charms with a wealth of thatched houses, some timber-framed with brick infilling, others colour-washed a deep cream. There wa̶ once an abbey here and Abbey Hous̶ stands opposite the church. The Tudo̶ south wing is claimed to be among th̶ earliest brick buildings in Dorset.

As the full walk forms a figure of eight you can easily choose a shortened route. Both sections include a stroll in the parkland surrounding Moor Crichel (sometimes spelt 'More Crichel') and a splendid view of Moor Crichel House, considered to be the finest Palladian mansion in Dorset. The longer walk then follows the valley of the Allen before climbing the down to Chalbury, famous for its 13th-century church crowning a fine viewpoint.

THE WALK

❶ From the car park, return to the road, turn left and walk through the village, passing the school on your left. When the road divides, keep ahead, signed 'Moor Crichel'. Follow the lane until it curves right in front of the gates at the entrance to Moor Crichel Park.

❷   Leave the lane, keep straight on through the right-hand gate and follow the metalled path through the Park. After about ¼ mile you will see the south front of Moor Crichel House overlooking a large lake with thickly wooded shores. Once a village stood here, but when Humphrey Sturt inherited Moor Crichel House in 1765, he swept the village away to make the present parkland and housed the

Chalbury church.

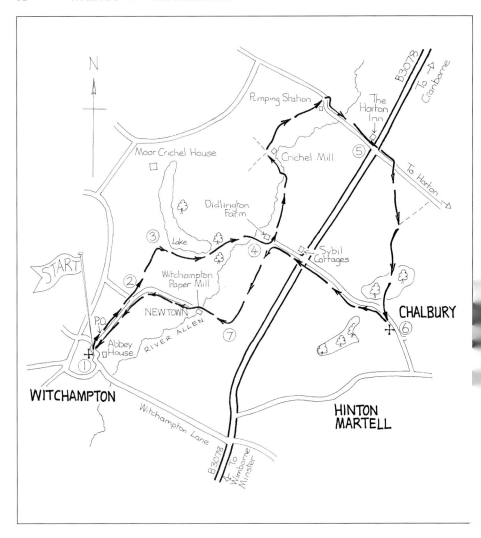

people in a settlement he called Newtown (seen later in the walk).

❸ At the 'private' sign turn right and follow the footpath with the lake at first on your left. The path continues through a white gate across open woodland. Continue over two bridges. The path bears right past Didlington Farm and a barn close

on the left to go through a gate to a crosstrack.

For the shorter walk: turn right here and follow the return route of the longer walk from Didlington Farm back to Witchampton.

❹ *For the longer walk:* turn left with the barn on the left to meet a lane. Bear right for a few yards then left, signed 'Stanbridge'. Keep ahead beside the river past a cottage on the left and follow the same track as it turns left over an iron-railed bridge and continues past Crichel Mill. Immediately after the Mill, turn right at the crossways and continue for about ½ mile to meet a road by a pumping station. Turn right beside the road and walk up to the Horton Inn on the skyline.

❺ By the inn you meet the main B3078. Turn left for a few yards then right up the lane signed 'Horton'. Continue for about 100 yards then turn right over a stile and follow the narrow path which leads half-left up the field to the top right-hand corner. Cross double stiles, turn right to cross another stile then bear half-left again to a stile just to the left of a conspicuous group of pine trees beside a house. Cross the stile to a track and turn right to leave the house on your right. Keep to this path as it bears left then winds uphill through woods to join an asphalted lane approaching Chalbury. Bear left, still uphill, to meet the lane running through the village. Turn left and follow the lane a little downhill, past private drives, to a flight of steps on the right leading uphill to

Chalbury's simple, whitewashed church, furnished in 18th-century style with box pews and large three-decker pulpit. Although the hill is only 335 feet high, the view north over Cranborne Chase and south to the hills of the Isle of Wight and the Needles is breathtaking.

❻ Descend the steps, turn left and follow the road past our previous access point on the right. The road goes down into the Allen valley to the main B3078 at Sybil Cottages. Cross straight over and follow the lane to Didlington. Turn left at the end of the lane to retrace our earlier route past the barn now on the right. (*The shorter route joins here.*) Do not turn right to retrace the route further but keep straight on along a wide grassy path for about ¾ mile.

❼ Turn right over the stile, cross the field ahead and go over a bridge to follow a narrow path to the right of Witchampton's early 18th-century paper mill. The path meets a lane in Newtown. Keep ahead along the lane which curves left to meet our outbound route by the gates to Moor Crichel Park. Retrace your steps along the road to Witchampton.

PAMPHILL

Length: 3 miles

Getting there: Pamphill is a mile west of Wimborne Minster. From Wimborne Minster take the B3082 in the direction of Blandford. Just after the Pamphill Dairy sign turn left for Pamphill, Cowgrove and Kingston Lacy church. Pass the Dairy Farm shop and restaurant

on the right and a lane to Pamphill Farm on the left and take the next left in front of the gates to the church to drive down an avenue of oak trees. If approaching from Blandford along the B3082, pass the entrance drive to Kingston Lacy House and shortly after turn

right for Pamphill.

Parking: Pass a car park on the right and continue to Pamphill Green car park on the left.

Map: OS Landranger 195. (GR 993004).

There is nowhere quite like Pamphill. As part of the vast Kingston Lacy Estate, now bequeathed to the National Trust but owned for many years by the Bankes family, the village has slumbered peacefully through the centuries almost untouched by time. Here there is no recognisable village street only a scattering of deep-thatched half-timbered cottages and farms set among the open greens of a still medieva

From Pamphill, the walk descends into the Stour valley and follows the riverside before crossing an ancient common to the small group of historic homesteads at Cowgrove. An attractive sunken path leads back to the village.

THE WALK

❶ Leaving the car park sign on the left and the sports field on your right walk down the lane ahead. On the left you pass an unusual building now Pamphill First School. Endowed by Roger Gillingham, it was built in 1698 with a school in the higher classical centre flanked by eight single-room almshouses. The lane divides in front of Pamphill Green. Take the left-hand lane and just past the Vine Inn car

landscape. History lies round every corner. Abbot Street Copse conceals the embankments of the first 'Kingston', a royal residence built by the Saxon King Ine in the 6th century. Nearby is a circular Saxon 'moot', an open air court room, and many of the cottages retain their Saxon names.

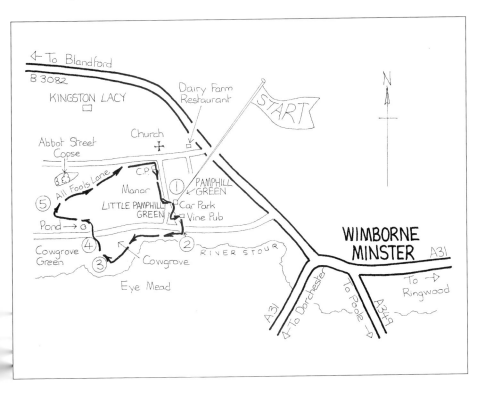

Cowgrove pond, near Pamphill.

park turn right to see Little Pamphill Green, a delectable group of cottages with beautiful views over the Stour valley. Bear left to leave the cottages on your right to complete a circle and return to the lane opposite the Vine Inn. We were surprised to see that the houses in this tiny place were numbered in the five hundreds. Evidently the Bankes family numbered all the houses on their estate consecutively and as their lands extended to the Purbecks, number one is in Studland! Turn right to leave the Vine Inn on your left and continue down the lane to a road.

❷ Cross the road and the stile ahead, and turn right with the Stour over the meadow on your left. Walk along the field edge, past a house on the right, to cross another stile.

Keep ahead to the next stile by a gate. Cross over and turn left to the riverside at Eye Mead. An information panel describes life here in Roman and medieval times. Do not cross the bridge but turn right to follow a grassy path beside the Stour which continues over a small wooden bridge close to the river bank. Follow the river for about ½ mile to a stile by a gate. Ahead the path narrows to run through a wood.

PLACES of INTEREST

Kingston Lacy is a magnificent mansion with a fine collection of paintings. Telephone: 01202 883402 for details of opening times and special events. **Badbury Rings**, a fine Iron Age hill fort off the B3082, 3 miles north-west of Pamphill, is well worth a visit.

❸ Cross the stile and turn right away from the river along a narrow path with a wire fence on the right. If you wish you could follow another parallel path on the left. The path winds north beside the fence past some ancient oak trees. Continue over a wooden walkway and take the parallel path as the narrow path is overgrown from this point. Cross a second wooden walkway and go over the stile to the edge of Cowgrove Common. Follow the path ahead over the green with a tiny stream on your right to meet a lane in Cowgrove. A thatched half-timbered house is on your right and opposite is Poplar Farm.

❹ Turn left for a few yards to Cowgrove Pond. Bear right round the pond to leave it on your left along a track marked with a footpath sign leading right and a blue bridleway sign indicating the gravel track straight ahead. Keep ahead, following the bridleway sign along the good track which runs past a cottage on the right and continues over an open green to pass a house on the right.

❺ Just past the house turn right, signed 'All Fools Lane'. This path dates from Saxon times and was originally 'All Souls Lane'. It led past King Ine's residence to a chapel at the top of the hill. The path leads through two sets of double gates. After the second set you will see Abbot Street Copse on the left, the site of the royal residence. Just before you meet a lane at the top of the hill turn right over the grass to cut the corner. Follow the lane for about 100 yards then bear right over the grass towards the oak avenue in Pamphill. Cross the car park and walk over the sports field past Pamphill Manor on the right towards the thatched cricket pavilion. Pamphill Green car park is on the left.

CRANBORNE

Length: 4½ miles

Getting there: Cranborne is 10 miles north of Wimborne Minster on the B3078. Heading north from Wimborne Minster, drive into the village and at the T-junction opposite the Sheaf of Arrows pub turn right, signed for the car park. After about 50 yards, before the road turns left, drive straight ahead into the car park.

Parking: In the car park as directed above.

Map: OS Landranger 195. (GR 055135).

Once Cranborne was a bustling market town, the capital of the Chase, a vast hunting forest covering over 100 square miles of chalk downland marking the borders of Wiltshire and Dorset. Today, it is a quiet village folded in the beautifully wooded valley of the river Crane.

Overlooking its attractive cluster of red brick houses is the church of St Mary and St Bartholomew, rebuilt in the 13th century and decorated with medieval wall paintings. From the churchyard there is a fine view of Cranborne Manor. Part of the manor dates back to Tudor times but it was

---

FOOD and DRINK

There are two pubs in Cranborne, the Sheaf of Arrows (telephone: 01725 517456) and the Fleur de Lys (telephone: 01725 517282). Both serve good food and ales.

---

greatly altered in the 17th century by the Cecil family, who still own the village.

If you enjoy walking in ancient oak woods this pleasant circuit will have a special appeal. Many of the great trees that once covered the whole of the Chase remain around Cranborne. The walk follows the valley of the Crane before returning along a terraced path giving wide views over the undulating countryside.

THE WALK

❶ With your back to the car park, follow the metalled path that runs to the left of the little river Crane. Pass a bridge on the right, and just before the path bears left, turn right over the second bridge to walk up to a road. Turn left and after about 200 yards, as the road bears left, turn right up a lane.

❷ A few yards up the lane you will see a stile on the left. Cross the stile and follow the path up a field towards the wooded

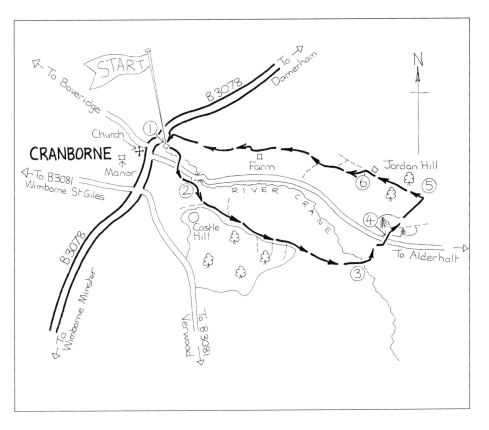

Cranborne Manor.

hillside. Crowning the crest of Castle Hill on the right are the embankments of an Iron Age fort. Climb the stile which leads to a track running along the edge of the woods and turn left to follow this beautiful path sunk between high banks, carpeted with wild flowers and shaded by old oaks and beeches. Continue past a path on the left and a deep hollow on the right to a fork. Keep ahead down the left-hand path, still tracing the edge of the woods. The path climbs through woods on either side then descends past a track on the right and continues to a crosstrack. Bear left down the left-hand track which now follows the edge of the wood and descends to run to the right of the river and cross a tributary stream. Cross a second stream and you will see a wooden bridge on the left.

❸ Turn left over the bridge which crosses a small weir. Bear left up a wide track to leave a house on the left and continue to a lane. Turn right to meet a road. Bear right up the road for about 30 yards to a footpath sign on the left.

❹ Leave the road and turn left to go through a gate into pine woods. The path climbs through the trees and bears right

PLACES of INTEREST

Cranborne Manor Garden Centre is well worth a visit. Opening times do vary so it is advisable to check first. The superb gardens themselves are open on Wednesdays from April to October and occasionally at other times. Telephone: 01725 517248 for details.

past a narrower path on the left. Continue along the main track as it winds uphill to a fork by a footpath sign. Leave the main path and take the left-hand path straight uphill to a more cleared area on the right. Follow the path to the right of trees to a footpath sign in front of a field. We saw no clear path at this point but navigation presents no problems. Look across the field to a gate in the opposite hedge a little to your right and walk up the field to go through the gate and join a wide grassy crosstrack.

❺ Turn left to follow another beautiful way bordered by massive oaks. Some of these veterans must have witnessed scenes from the days when the Chase was a royal playground. Gaily dressed parties of huntsmen must have galloped beneath their branches and furtive bands of poachers and fugitives hidden in their shade. The path rises to the top of Jordan Hill in front of a house. Just past the house look for a grassy way on the left leading to a stile by a gate.

❻ Cross the stile and follow the path as it curves left along the hillside with woods close on the right. When the woodland ceases continue downhill to a crosspath in front of a hedge. Bear left, hedge on right, for a few yards to two stiles. Turn right over the stile to follow a field path along the valley with a hedge on the left towards a farm. On the hill beyond the farm you will see the tower of Cranborne church. Pass the farm on your left and continue ahead to a lane. Bear right for a few yards then turn left over a stile to continue with a hedge on the left. This leads to a road running past the first houses in Cranborne on the left and the sports field on the right to meet the main B3078. Turn left to return to the car park which is on the left.

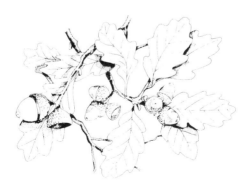